Contents

Symbols used in this guide

1 Roman site
(visible remains)

2 Roman site
(no visible remains)

Roman wall/quay
(no visible remains)

Line of Roman bridge
(no visible remains)

3 *Speculative* Roman site
or artefact

4 Iron-age site/person
(no visible remains)

4 Modern artefact
inspired by the Romans

A Museum
(with Roman artefacts)

A Ancient river/stream
(no visible remains)

Modern extent of
River Thames

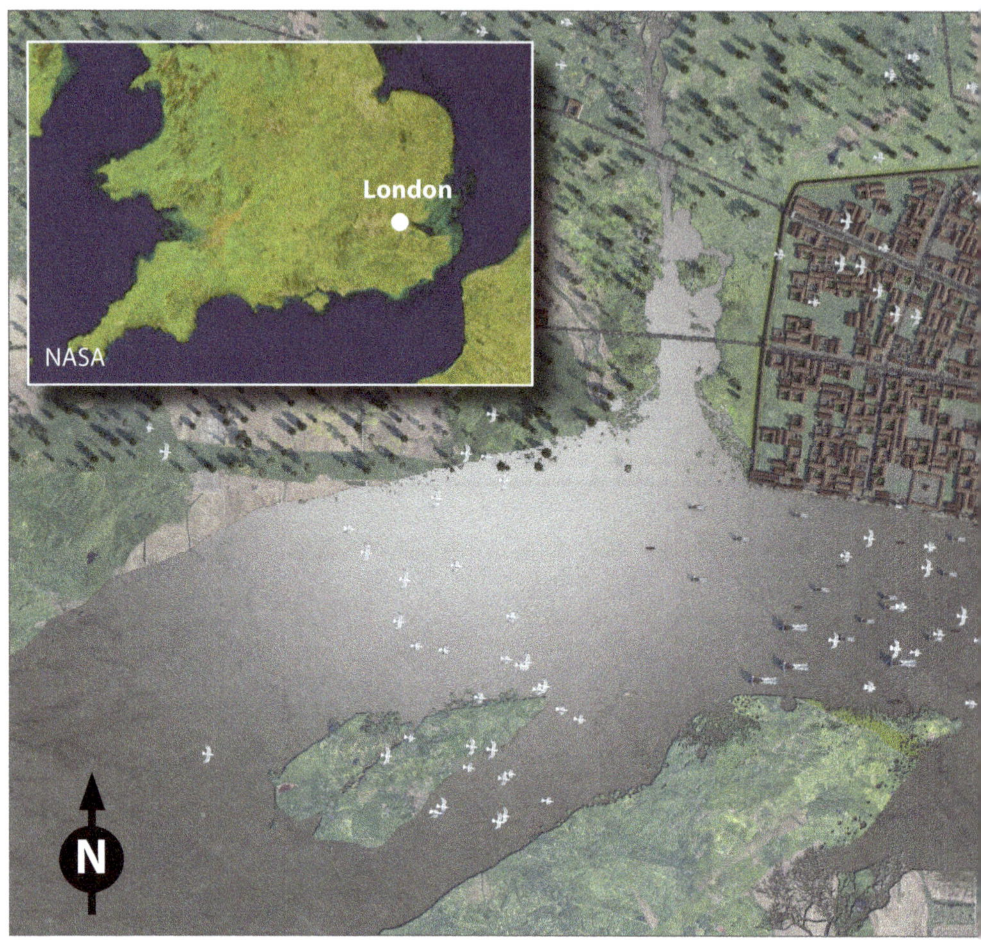

A speculative view of London, looking north, 245 CE.

Introduction

London has a long and complex history, spanning almost two thousand years. This guide explores how London evolved from 30 CE to 245 CE. In this time it changed from marshland to the capital of Roman Britain. After this date the Roman Empire started a gradual decline and by 410 CE Britain was under constant attack by marauding Anglo-Saxons.

Trade continued to be the lifeblood of London, allowing it to develop into one of the centres for global commerce it has become today.

The guide features full-colour reconstructions all looking north, showing key points in Roman London's history and important sites such as the Amphitheatre and Mithraeum. Modern maps allow you to compare the past with present day London.

Changing archaeology

The text and illustrations in this guide are based on a significant amount of research. But archaeology is constantly evolving and certain sites may in the future be reinterpreted. One example, is a large palace (see page 44), which was thought to belong to the Governor of Roman Britain, which is now thought to have been a large Bathhouse.

So this guide is based on the 'current' view of how Roman London may have been.

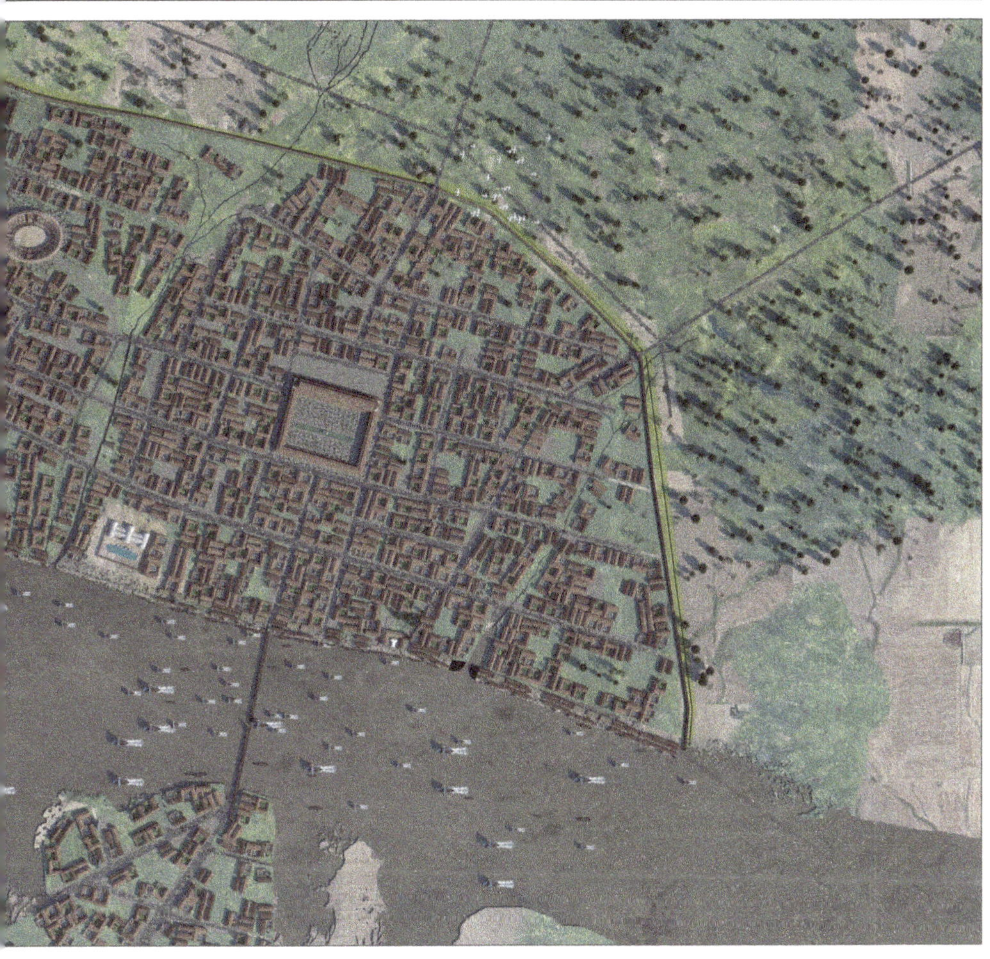

The Romans

The city of Rome in central Italy was formed around 800 BCE and grew over the centuries into the Roman Empire, which covered most of Europe, the Middle East and North Africa. It was a highly sophisticated and technologically advanced society, with a huge army, major roads and large cities. Britain at that time was a mysterious place with fierce tribes and valuable metals, which became the focus of two attempted invasions in 55 BCE and 54 BCE by *Julius Caesar*. Those invasions were repelled by local tribes and the Romans did not try again to invade Britain for almost 100 years. By 43 CE the *Emperor Claudius (who needed the army's support)* decided to invade Britain. After first attacking Colchester, via the London area, the Emperor's forces then moved across England including back to where the present day City of London is located...

Visiting Roman London

Roman London lies in an area called the City of London, which is located in the east side of modern London, north of the Thames. There are many museums with Roman artefacts inside this area.

Just outside this area are many fine museums, including the British Museum and the London Museum, due to open late 2026.

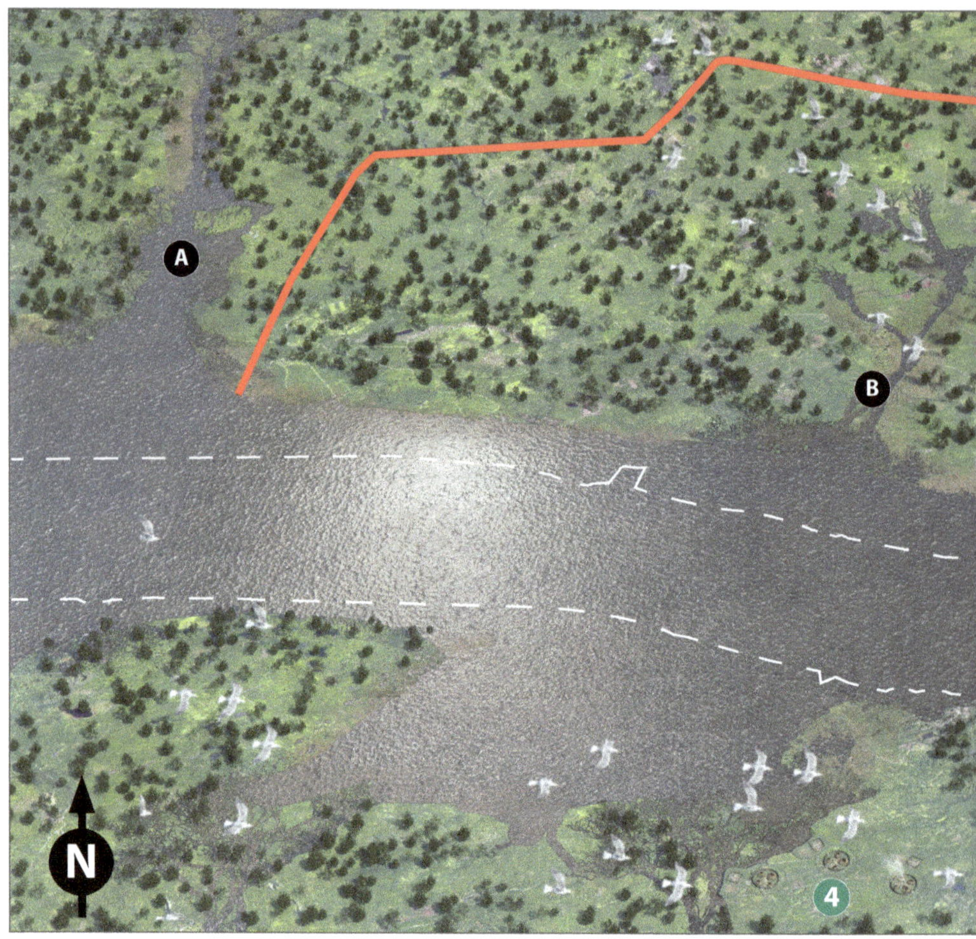

A speculative view of London, looking north, 30 CE.

London 30 CE

Before the Roman invasion, the area which became London was woodland and marshes, with the River Thames cutting through the middle. At some points the Thames could be up to 1000 m *(3000 ft)* wide, depending on the tides.

The river acted as a buffer zone between the increasingly hostile tribes in the Hertfordshire/Essex area[1] and the pro-Roman tribes in the Hampshire/Kent area[2]. Around 30 CE the area was mostly empty except for a few scattered Iron Age roundhouses. The origin of the name *'London'* is not known exactly, although it may have come from an Iron Age word: *Londonion*, possibly meaning *the fort by the lake*.

The precise meaning is not known and could have just referred to a general area, rather than a specific place.

1. *The Catuvellauni and the Trinovantes.*
2. *The Atrebates and the Cantiaci.*

Key

— *Future Roman Walls*
A *River Fleet*
B *Walbrook Stream*
C *Lorteburn Stream*
4 *Iron Age site*

Find out more

The River Fleet, Walbrook Stream and Lorteburn Stream, now no longer visible, are shown on the map with the ghosted blue sections and the black circles.

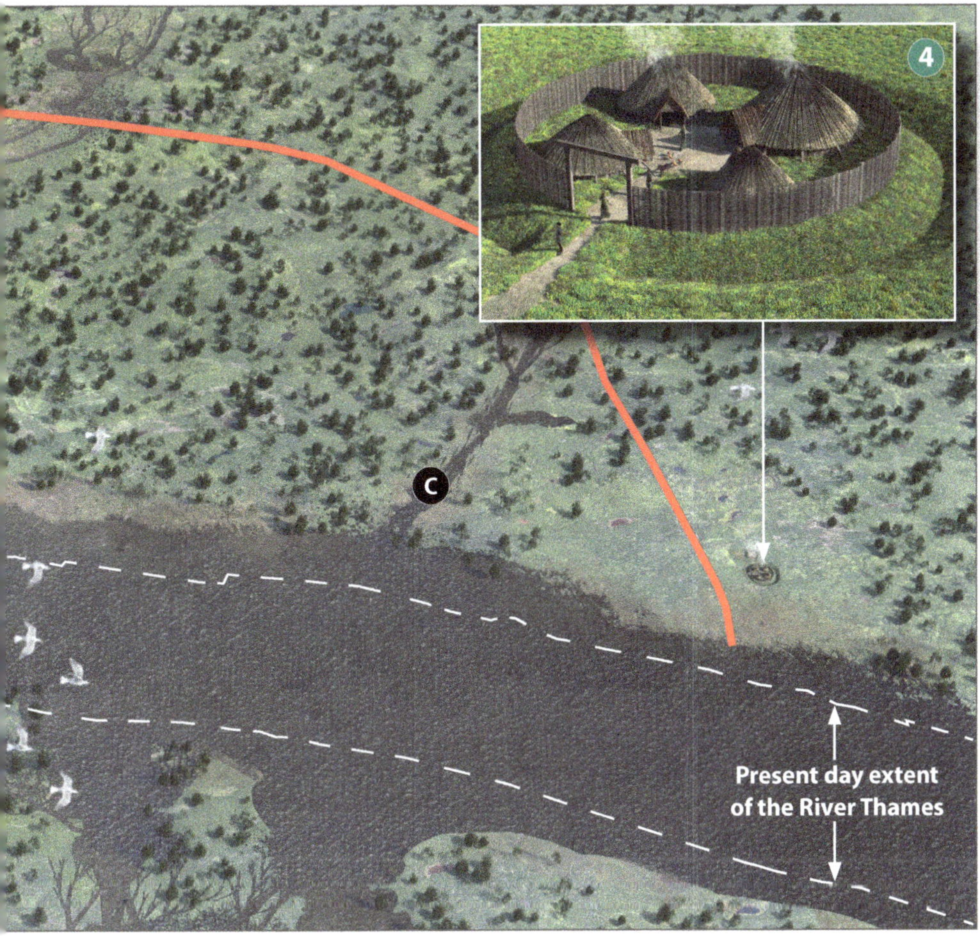

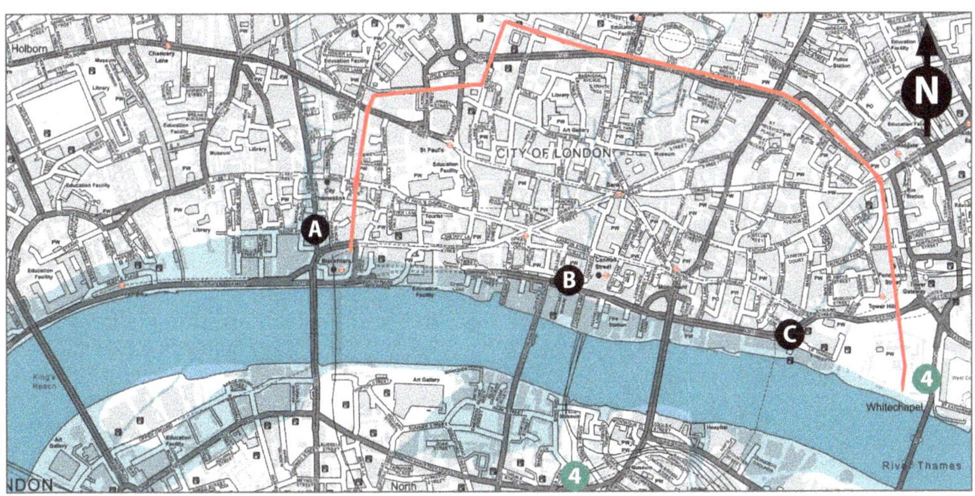

Contains Ordnance Survey data © Crown copyright and database right 2026

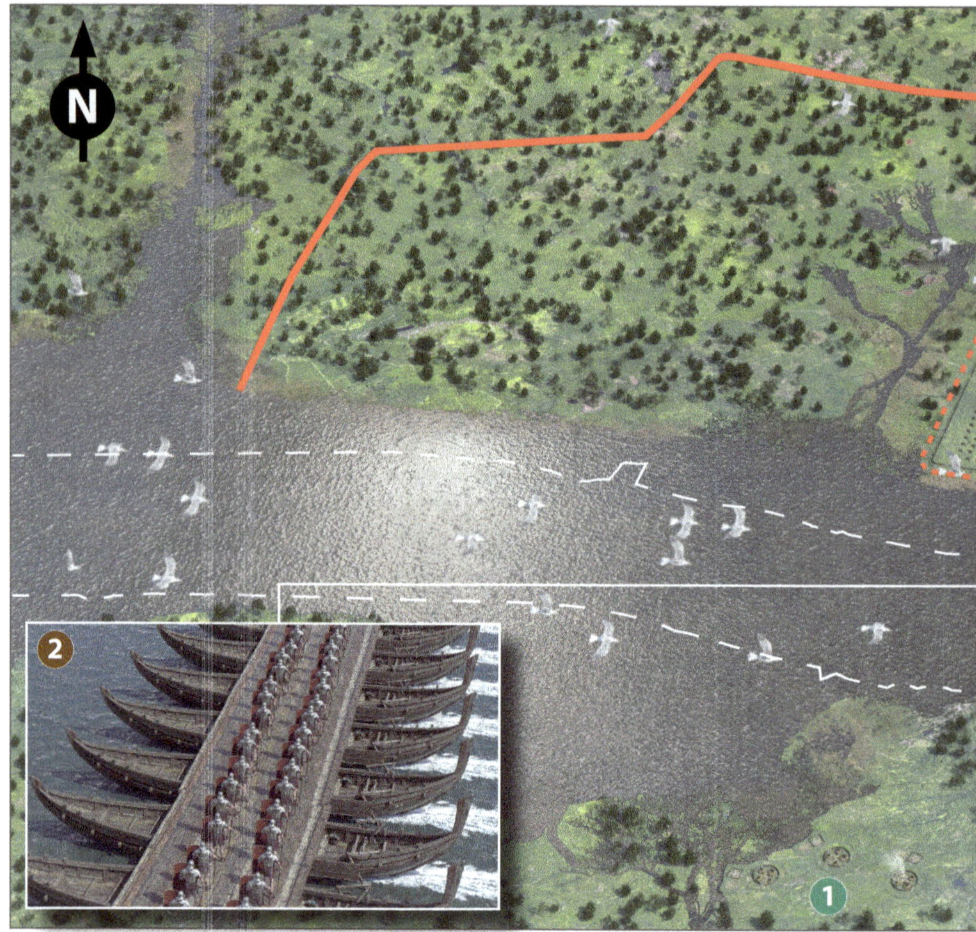

A speculative view of London, looking north, 43 CE.

London 43 CE

In 43 CE the Romans invaded England, targeting *Camulodunum (Colchester)* in Essex. They struggled to cross the Thames and were slowed by hit-and-run attacks from the local tribes who knew the area. It is possible that once the initial crossing had been achieved the Romans constructed a pontoon bridge to speed up the movement of troops and supplies. The Romans then waited for a few weeks for Emperor Claudius to arrive, before marching together towards the major Iron Age settlement of *Camulodunum*[1]. The Romans built a large temporary fortified area, north of the Thames. This might have been done while the Romans waited for the Emperor. Roman soldiers often built temporary camps called *castra*, while inside hostile areas, although this one was larger than a typical castra.

1. Just outside present day Colchester.

Key

— Future Roman Walls

▪ ▪ Extent of temporary fortified area

1 Iron Age site

2 Speculated Roman Pontoon Bridge[2]

3 Legionary tents

2. A pontoon bridge is made up of boats lashed together.

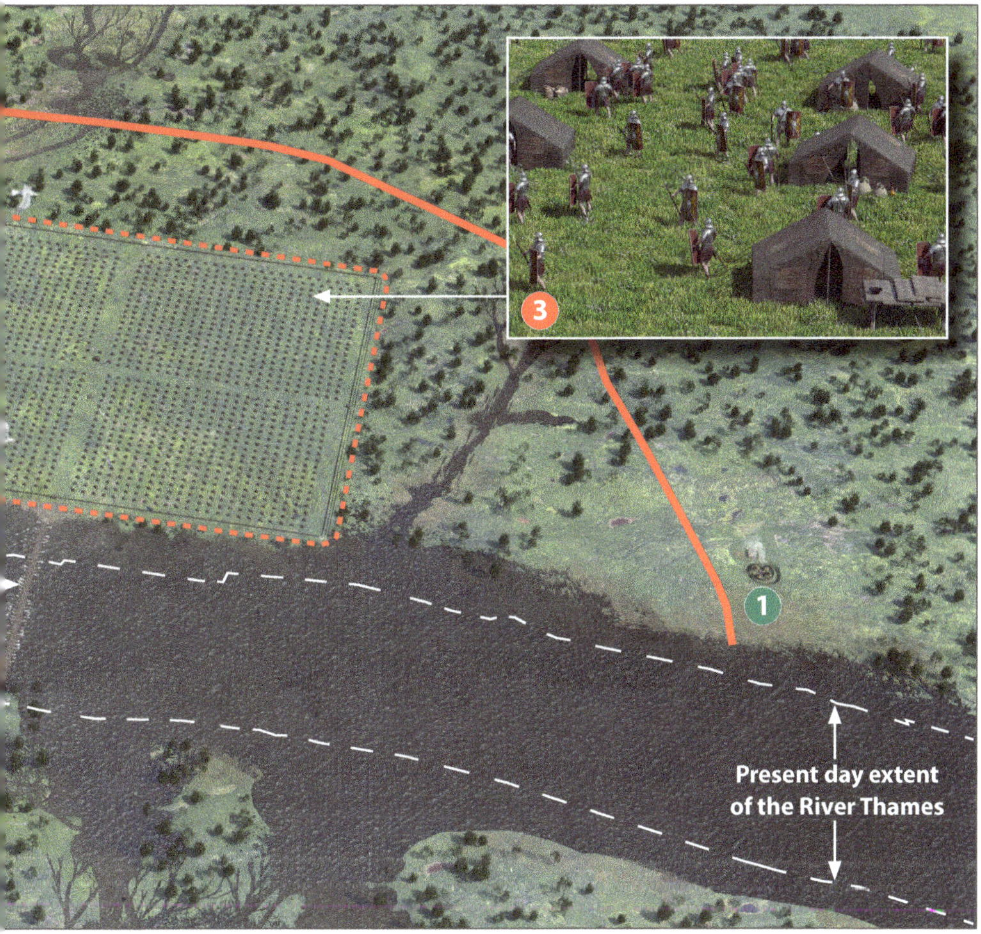

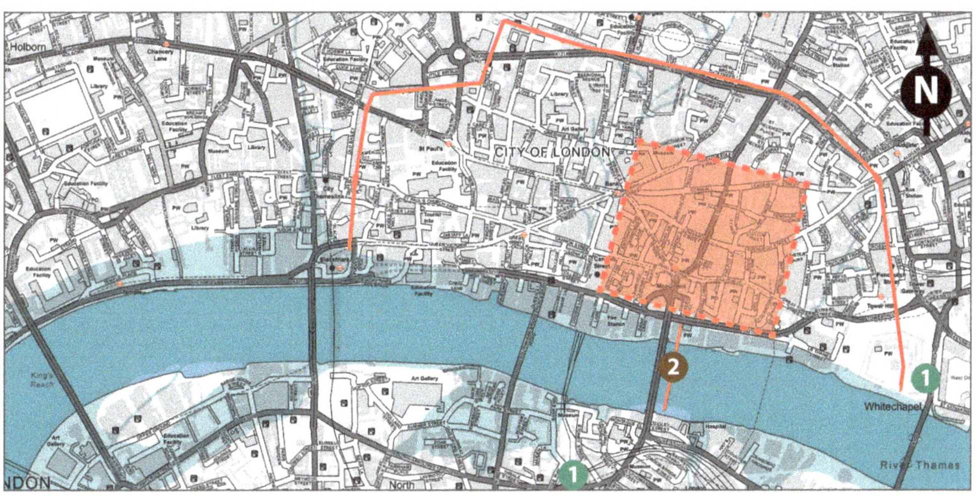

Contains Ordnance Survey data © Crown copyright and database right 2026

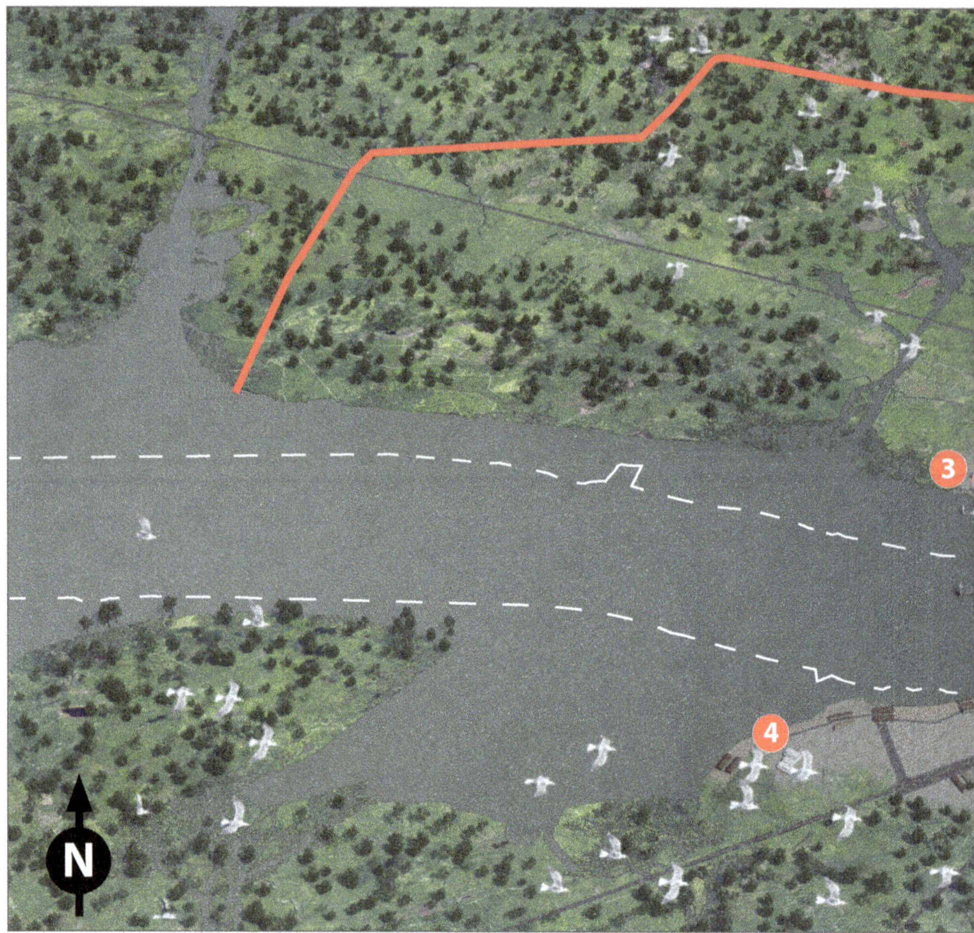

A speculative view of London, looking north, 55 CE.

London 55 CE

Camulodunum (Colchester) was the first capital of Roman Britain, while London was at this time a small supply base. By 50 CE a network of roads was started in the south-east of England, including through the area which is now the City of London[1]. At that time a small trading settlement was starting to be built, along with a ferry to cross the River Thames. The Thames had a major advantage for the Romans in that it was deep enough to allow seagoing ships far inland. Within a few years a wooden bridge had been built across the river, allowing an even better connection with the road network. By 60 CE London was a bustling area full of traders mostly supplying the Roman Army, with much activity around an early Forum area, in the centre of the town.

1. *The City of London refers broadly to the area covered in this book, but not the whole of London.*

Key

- Future Roman Walls
1. *Early Forum*
2. *Wooden bridge[2]*
3. *Revetments for basic quay*
4. *Bathhouse*
5. *Stores and offices*

2. *Probably by this time a wooden bridge crossed the Thames. It is thought that the ships had to lower their masts to allow them to travel past the bridge.*

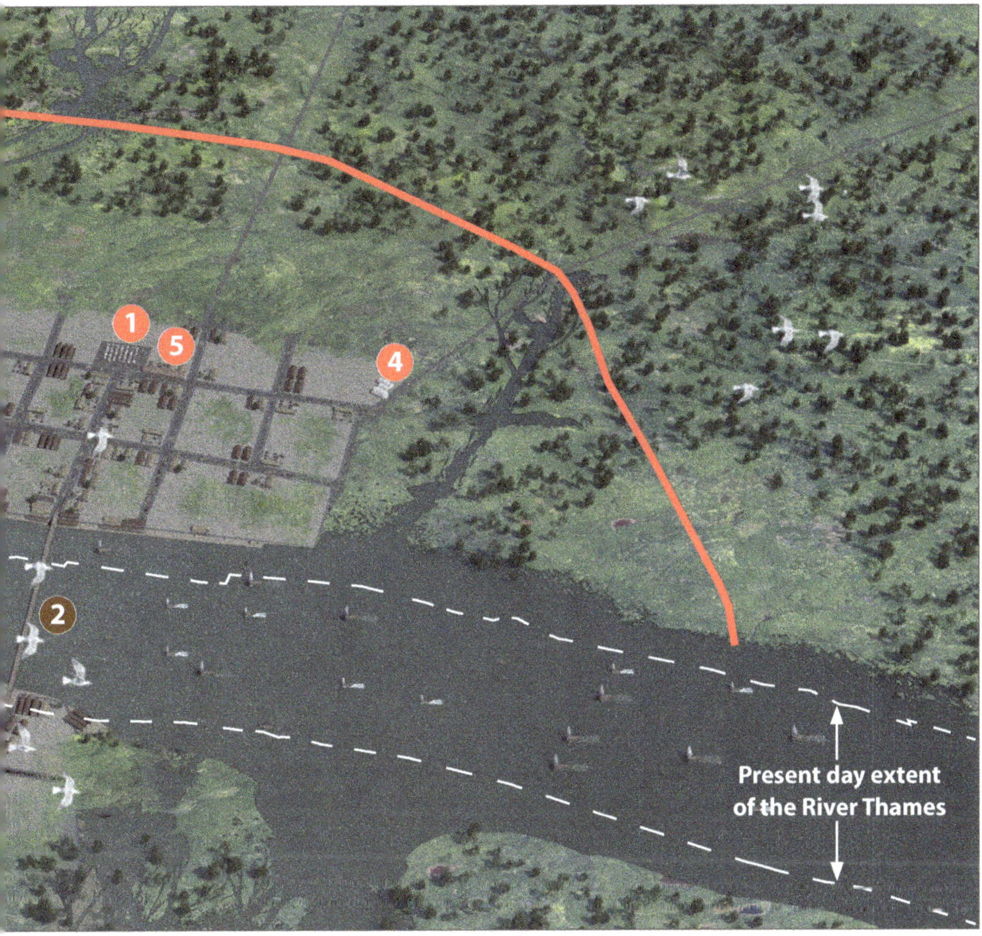

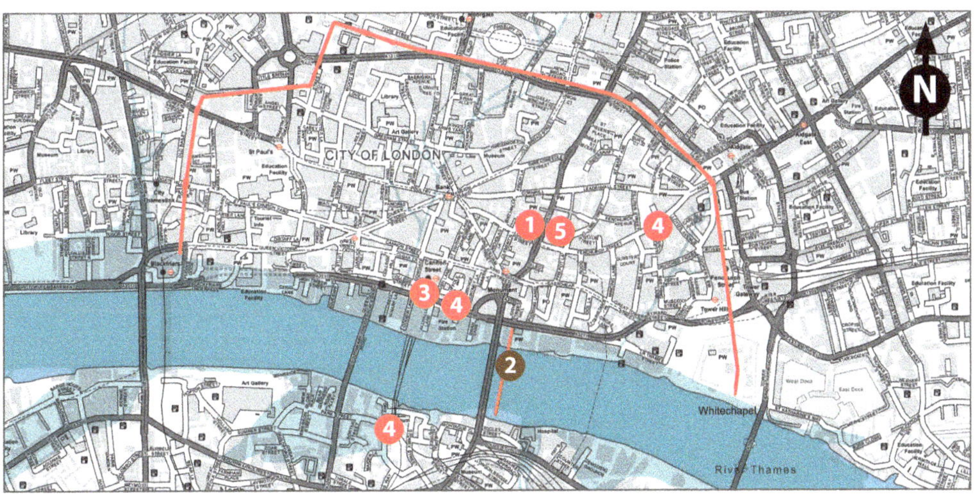

Contains Ordnance Survey data © Crown copyright and database right 2026

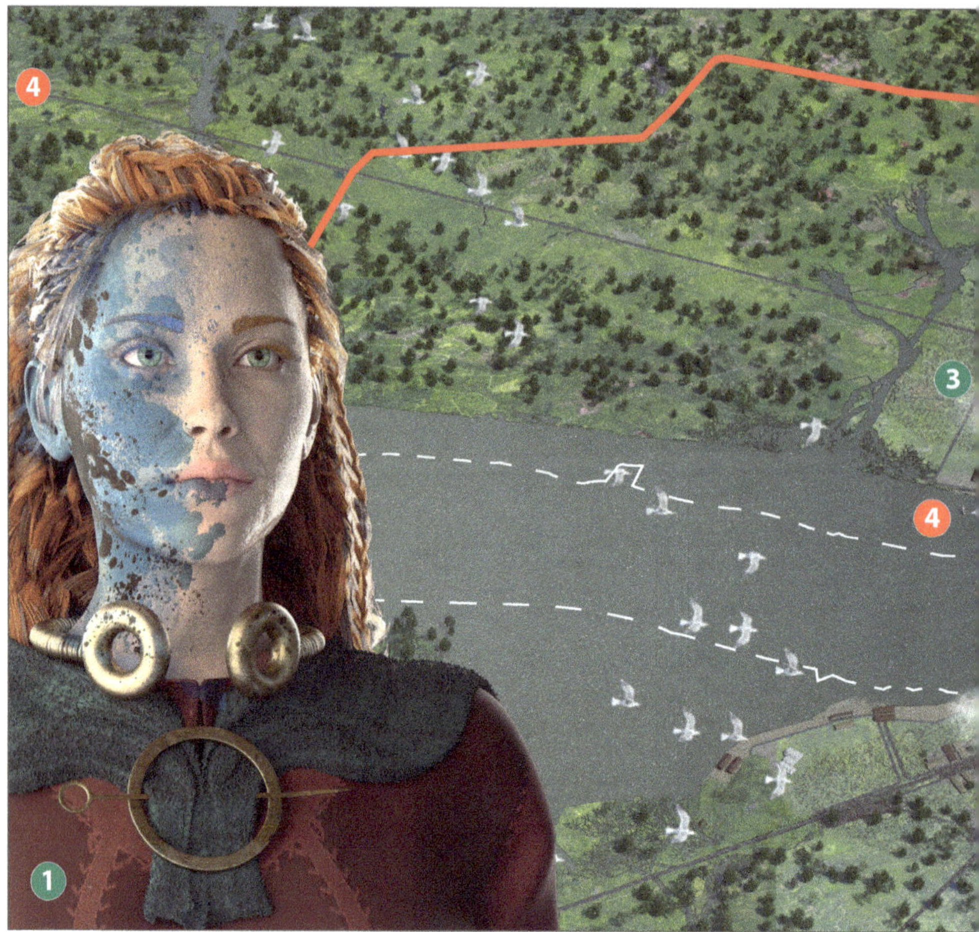

A speculative view of London and Boudica, looking north, 60/61 CE.

Boudica attacks London

In 60/61 CE the *Iceni*[1] mounted a rebellion against the occupying Roman forces. The *Iceni* led by Queen *Boudica*[2] swept south, gathering around 120,000 warriors, including some from other tribes. Their first target was the capital of Roman Britain: Colchester. *Boudica* and her forces then moved south towards *Londinium (London)*. The Governor of Roman Britain, *Gaius Suetonius Paulinus,* decided that he would be unable to defeat the *Iceni*, due to a lack of soldiers, so he left London to its fate. He allowed anyone who could do so to leave with him, but everyone else had to face the full force of *Boudica's* attack. London was burnt to the ground, with *Boudica* then moving north towards St. Albans.

1. *A tribe that ruled the area roughly covered by Norfolk.*
2. *There are different spellings of Boudica/Boudicca/Boadicea that have been used since Roman times.*

Key

- ▬ *Future Roman Walls*
- ① *Boudica*[3]
- ② *Burning buildings*
- ③ *Iceni warriors*
- ④ *Fleeing residents*

3. *The illustration above includes a speculative view of how Boudica might have looked. Her jewellery is based on those found in Norfolk, that can be seen in The British Museum.*

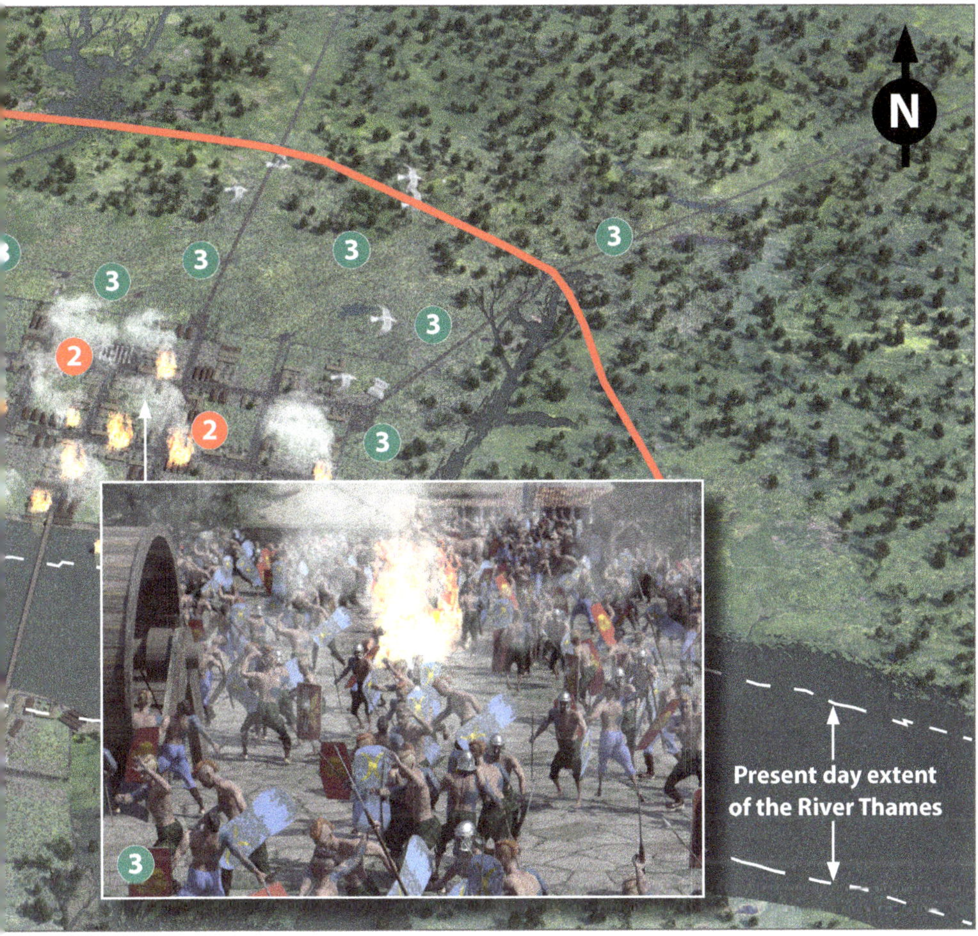

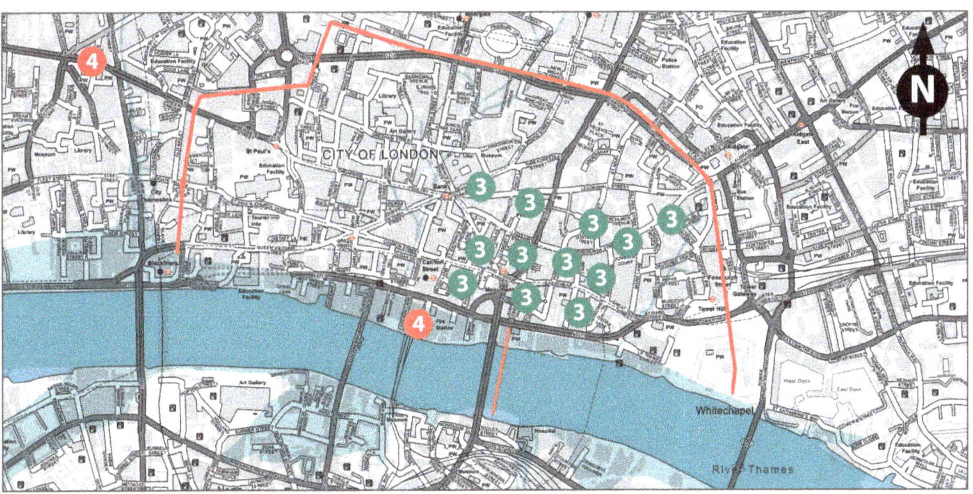

N
3
3
3
3
3
3
2
2
3
3
Present day extent
of the River Thames

N
4
CITY OF LONDON
3
4
Whitechapel
River Thames

A speculative view of London, looking north, 130 CE.

London 130 CE

By this time London had undergone decades of rapid development, going from the burnt-out ruins[1] of a small trading port to the new capital of Roman Britain. A fortress had also been established, as well as a large number of public buildings including a Basilica/Forum, temples and an amphitheatre. London was now well connected with other towns including York, St. Albans and Silchester.

The docks had also been extended to cope with the increase in goods brought in by ship from across the Roman Empire. These goods included: military equipment, emeralds from Egypt, marble from Turkey, olive oil from Spain and much more. Goods produced in Roman Britain also left London for the rest of the Roman Empire including gold, silver and salt.

1. London also had another large fire around 127 CE, but it is not known what caused it.

Key

- Roman walls (including the future Roman Town Wall, *see overleaf*)
1. Amphitheatre (*see p. 16*)
2. Roman Fortress
3. Forum/Basilica (*see p. 20*)
4. Gov. Palace (*see p. 44*)
5. Road to Silchester
6. Road to St. Albans and Wroxeter
7. Road to Lincoln and York
8. Road to Colchester
9. Road to Richborough
10. Road to Chichester

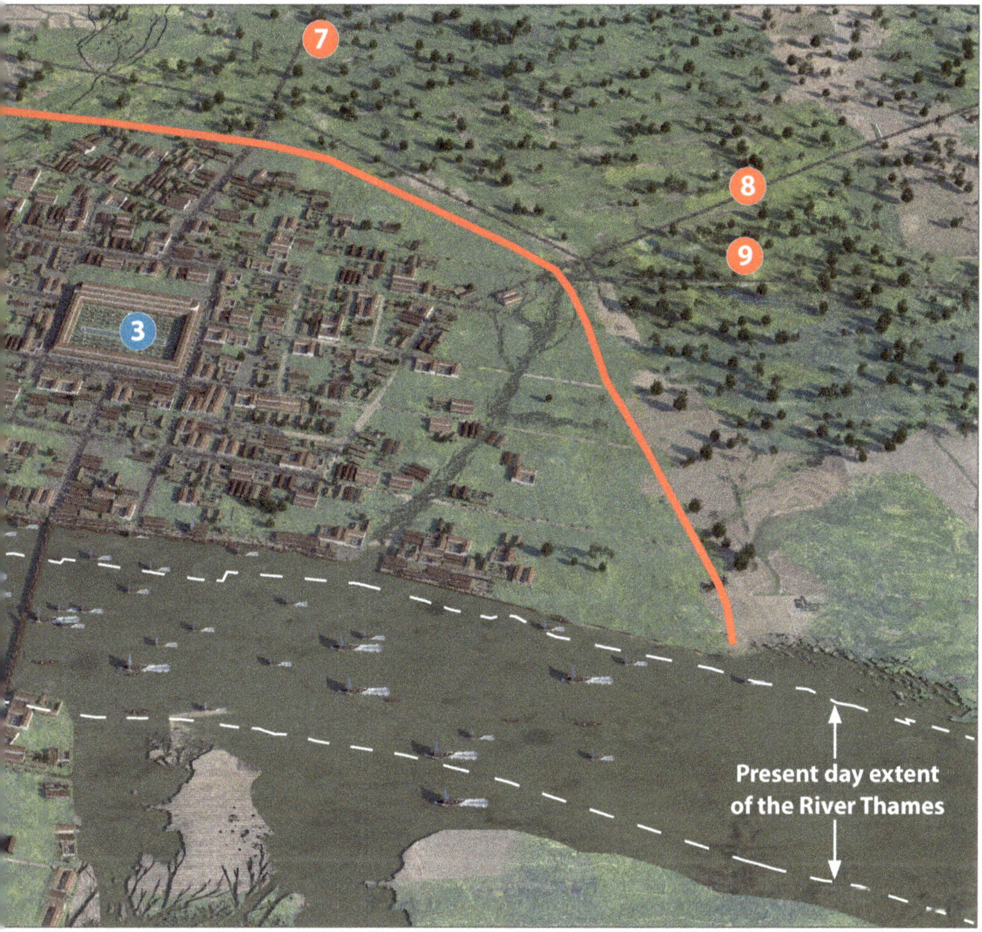

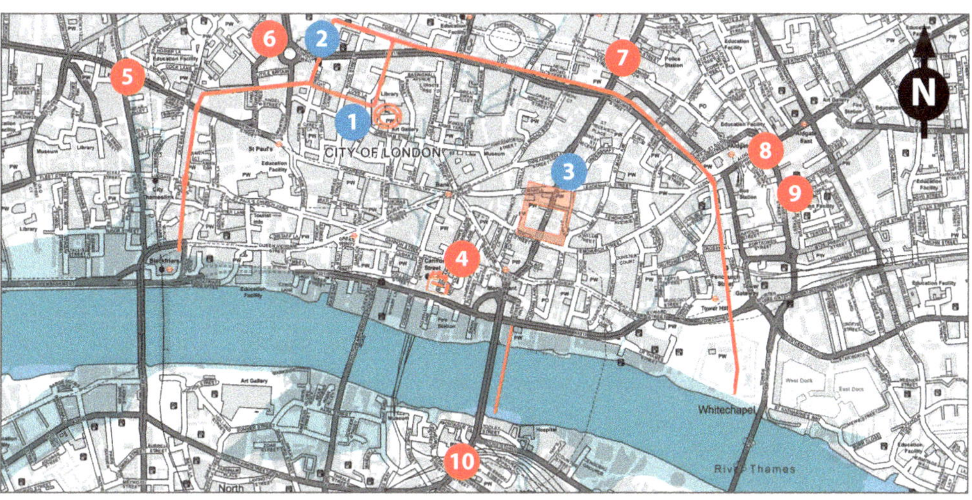

7
8
9
3
Present day extent
of the River Thames
6
2
5
7
1
CITY OF LONDON
St Paul's
3
8
9
4
N
Whitechapel
River Thames
North
10

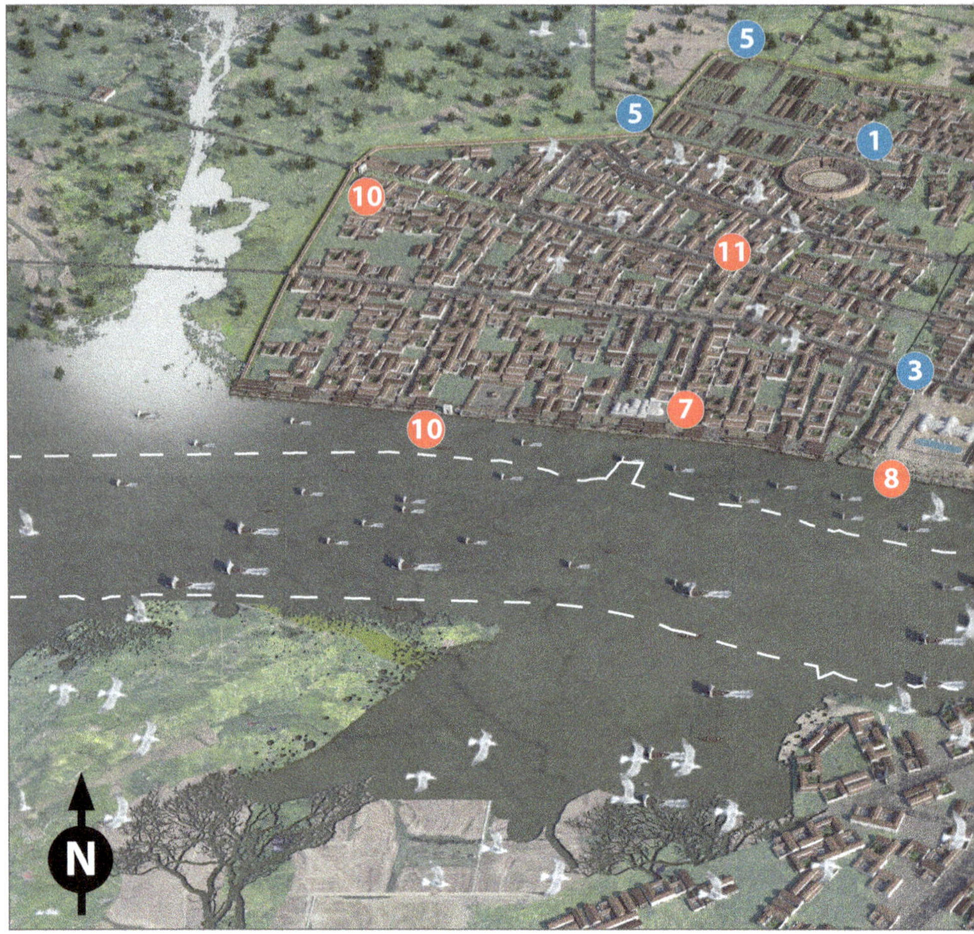

A speculative view of London, looking north, 245 CE.

London 245 CE

By this time the Roman Empire was gradually starting to crumble. *Dio Cassius (a Roman historian)* commented that the empire went *"from a kingdom of gold to one of rust and iron"*. There were still various public building works in progress, throughout London. These included the Mithraeum and one or more Triumphal arches. By around 220 CE a 6m *(19 ft)* wall surrounded most of the town[1]. In addition the fortress was abandoned, with the east and south walls having been demolished. Another major change for Roman London was how the port area was used. It was effectively blocked up with a new section of wall built by 350 CE. A possible reason for blocking the port may be linked to the level of the River Thames falling quite rapidly in the years since the invasion, making the port less useful than before.

1. Bastions were added to the wall in the fourth century, see p.22.

Key

- ▬ *Roman Town Wall (see p. 22)*
- ① *Amphitheatre (see p. 16)*
- ② *Basilica/Forum (see p. 20)*
- ③ *Mithraeum (see p. 18)*
- ④ *Roman Wall (see p. 22)*
- ⑤ *Abandoned Fortress*
- ⑥ *Roman Bridge (see p. 30)*
- ⑦ *'Huggin Hill' Public Bathhouse (see p. 44)*
- ⑧ *'Gov. Palace' (see p. 44)*
- ⑨ *Billingsgate Bathhouse (see page 24)*
- ⑩ *Possible Triumphal Arch*
- ⑪ *Cheapside Bathhouse (see page 42)*

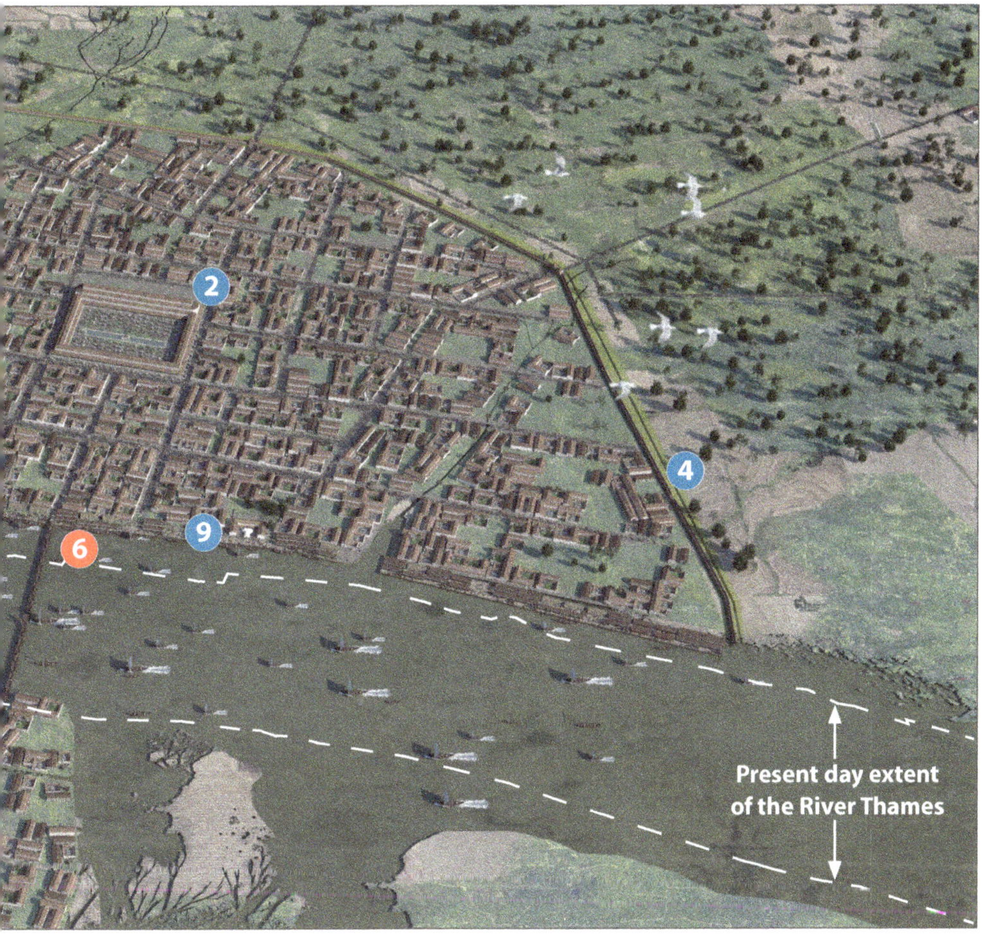

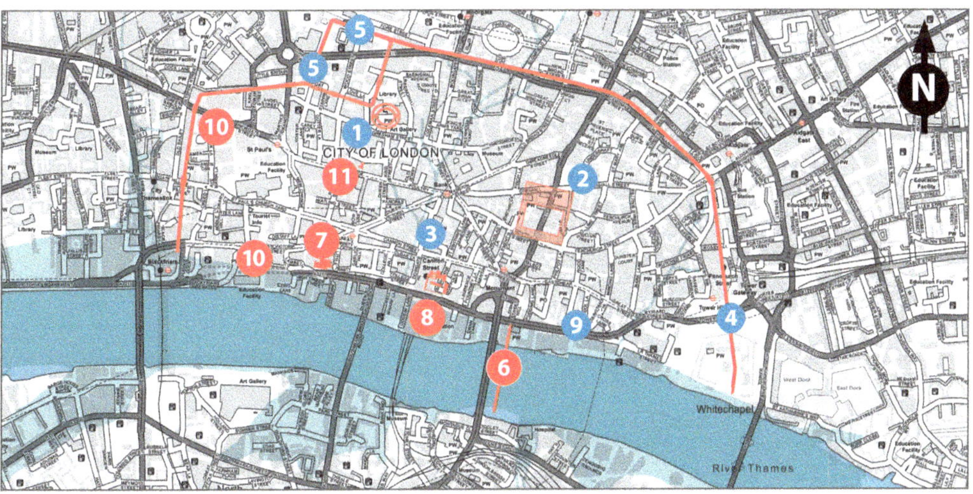

Contains Ordnance Survey data © Crown copyright and database right 2026

A speculative view of the amphitheatre, looking north, around 230 CE.

The Amphitheatre

In 1988 archaeologists discovered the remains of a massive amphitheatre in the Guildhall Yard, just off Gresham Street. The first amphitheatre, made from wood, was built around 70 CE. Around 110 CE the amphitheatre was upgraded with stone and a capacity for up to 10,500 people, all wanting a view of the gladiators fighting. Shops and stalls would have been clustered around the base of the amphitheatre, selling food to the crowds. Contests usually began with the gladiators *(Latin for swordsmen)* paraded in front of the crowd, with music playing. These contests often started in the morning, with the victors celebrated in the middle of the day. Bears, wolves, criminals and Christians were all forced to fight in the *'games'* held inside the amphitheatre.
The Roman Amphitheatre Guildhall Museum has extensive sections of the amphitheatre on display.

Key

- ▬ Amphitheatre/Roman Wall
- ① Amphitheatre
- ② Entrance
- ③ Gladiator
- ④ Seating/standing area
- ⑤ Area for dignitaries
- ⑥ Gatehouse ruins
- ⑦ Ruined fortress wall
- ⑧ Market stalls
- Ⓑ Walbrook Stream
- Ⓐ Roman Amphitheatre Guildhall Museum

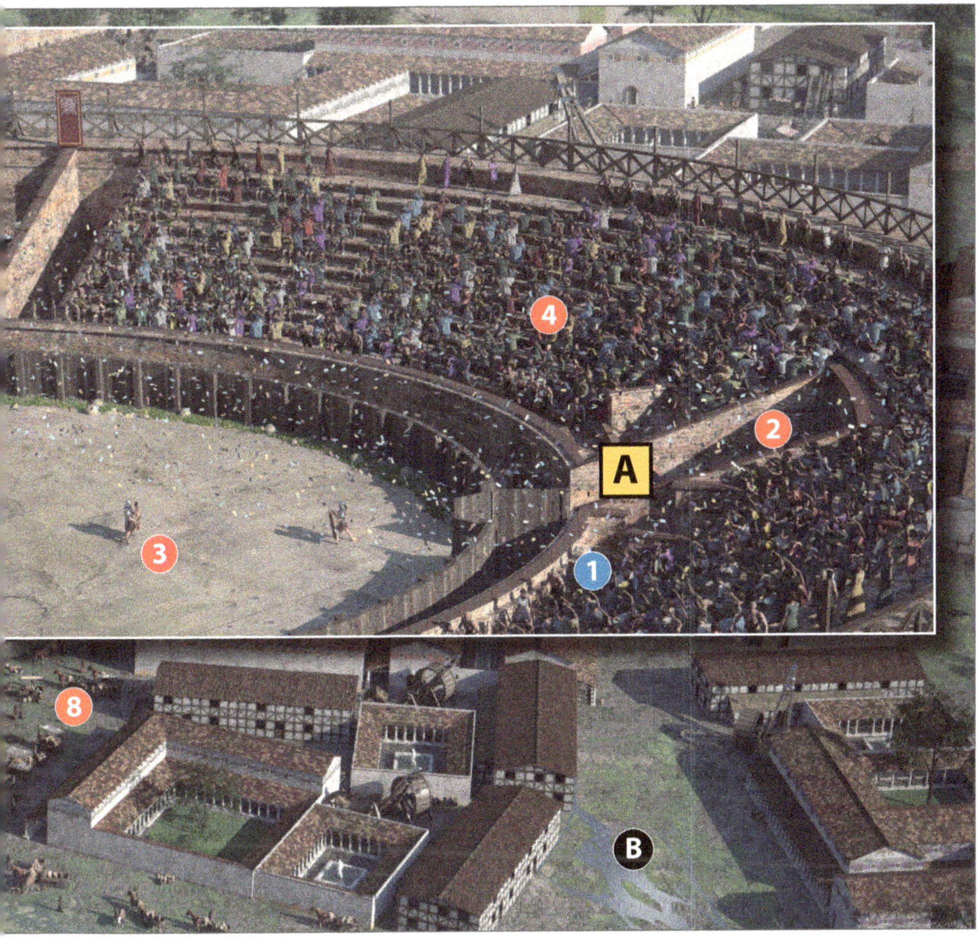

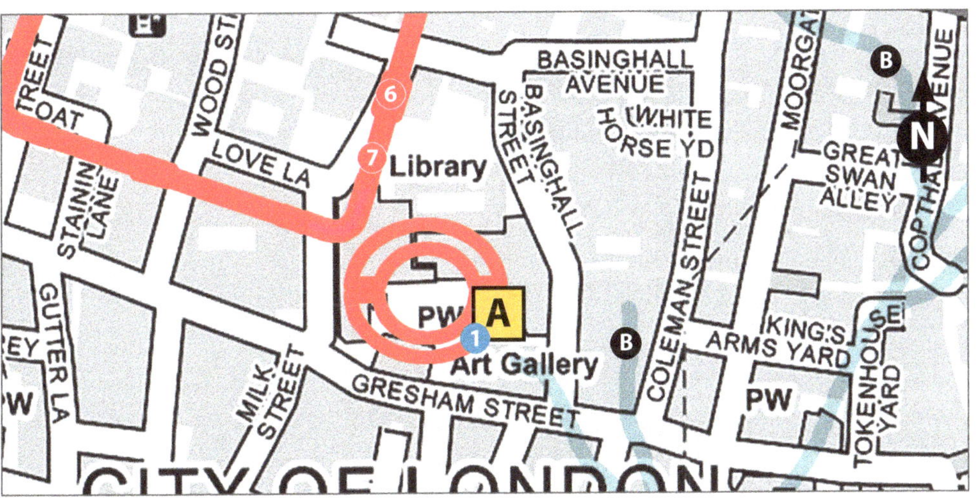

TREET
OAT
STAININ LANE
WOOD ST
LOVE LA
6
7 Library
BASINGHALL AVENUE
W.HITE HORSE YD
BASINGHALL STREET
MOORGATE
GREAT SWAN ALLEY
COPTHALL AVENUE
B
N
GUTTER LA
MILK STREET
PW
A
1
Art Gallery
GRESHAM STREET
COLEMAN STREET
B
KING'S ARMS YARD
PW
TOKENHOUSE YARD
CITY OF LONDON

A speculative view of the interior of the Mithraeum, around 245 CE.

The Mithraeum

In 1954 a *Mithraeum* was discovered by Professor *William Grimes*, as part of the task of recording sites in the City of London destroyed by bombs during the Second World War. The *Mithraeum* or Temple of *Mithras*[1] was built around 240 CE and may later have been reused as a temple dedicated to *Bacchus*[2]. Inside the temple there would have been initiation ceremonies and feasts. These possibly took place in the central nave, which was connected to an apse, where a cult statue of Mithras was placed.

1. *Unlike other Roman gods, there is little information about Mithras who was adapted by the Romans from a Middle Eastern religion, dating from around 1,400 BCE. The religion was popular amongst the military and was centred around Mithras killing a bull.*
2. *Bacchus was the Roman god of wine and fertility.*

Key

1 *Mithraeum*
2 *Central nave*
3 *Apse*
4 *Statue of Mithras*
5 *Statue*
6 *Astrological symbols*
B *Walbrook Stream*
B *London Mithraeum, Bloomberg SPACE Museum (see page 44)*

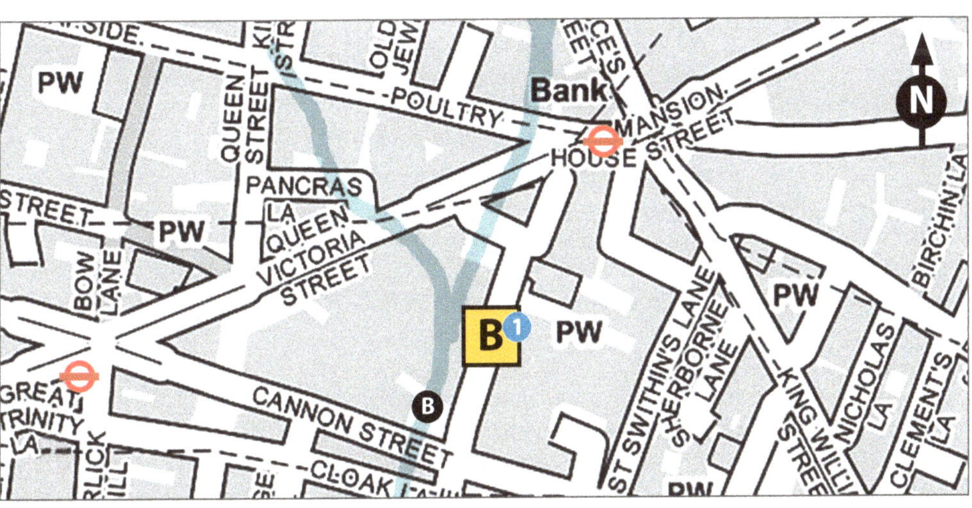
PW
QUEEN STREET
KI STR
OLD JEW
CE'S EET
POULTRY
Bank
MANSION
STREET
N
PANCRAS LA.
HOUSE STREET
STREET
PW
QUEEN
VICTORIA
STREET
BOW LANE
BIRCHIN LA.
B
PW
PW
GREAT TRINITY LA.
B
ST SWITHIN'S LANE
SHERBORNE LANE
PW
RLICK ILL
CANNON STREET
KING WILLI STREET
NICHOLAS LA.
CLEMENT'S LA.
CLOAK LA.
PW

A speculative view of the Basilica and Forum, looking north, 230 CE.

The Basilica and Forum

The *Basilica* and *Forum (public square)* were the most important civic structures in major Roman towns. The Basilica and Forum were first built in 75 CE and then a major upgrade was built around 120 CE. This new site was 170m *(557 ft)* long by 170m *(557 ft)* wide, making it the largest building in Roman London. The central section of the Basilica may have been 25m *(82 feet)* high, surrounded by high-status offices with painted walls. Part of the Basilica may have contained a raised platform where magistrates handed out judgements. The Forum was now a massive courtyard, possibly with a large ornamental pool. In addition there were large bronze statues, including one of Emperor Hadrian. Some of the items traded here could have included: Middle-Eastern dried fruit, Spanish seafood and German glassware, all of which have been found in Roman London.

Key

— Roman Wall
1 Upgraded Basilica[1]
2 Upgraded Forum
3 Ornamental pool
4 Bronze statue[2]
5 Market stalls
6 Bishopsgate (see p. 22)

1. See page 42 for details about viewing the upgraded Basilica.
2. The head of the statue of the Emperor Hadrian can be seen in the British Museum.

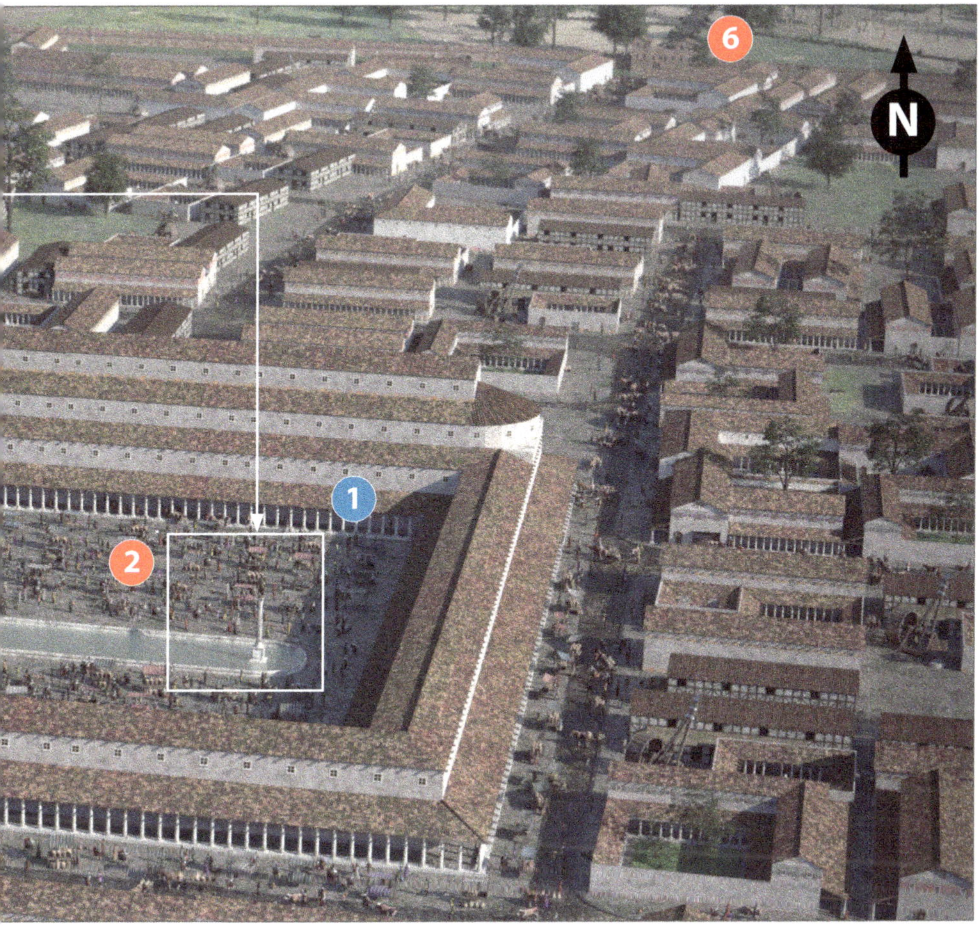

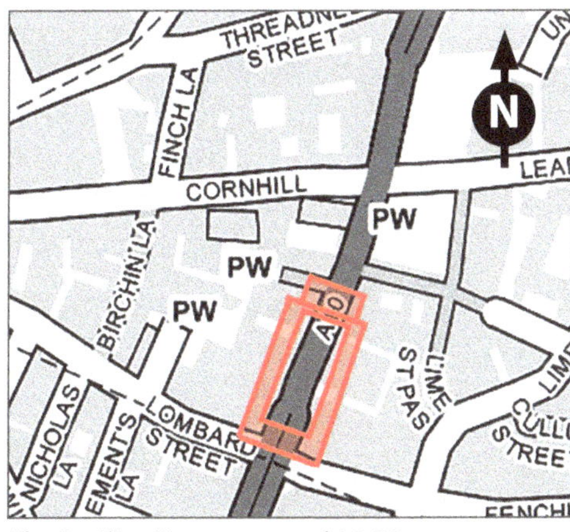

The Basilica/Forum around 85 CE.

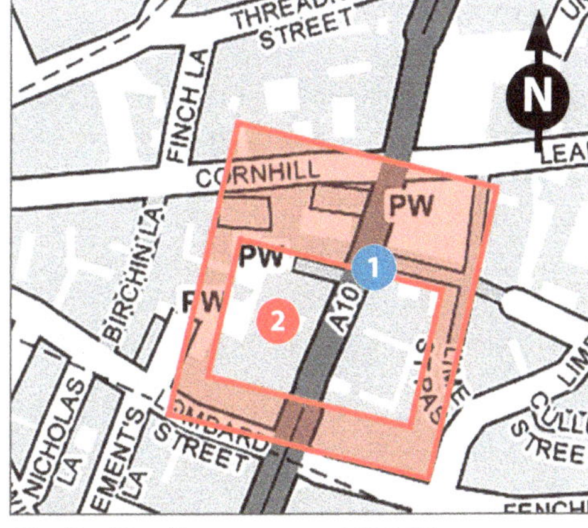

The Basilica/Forum around 120 CE.

Contains Ordnance Survey data © Crown copyright and database right 2026

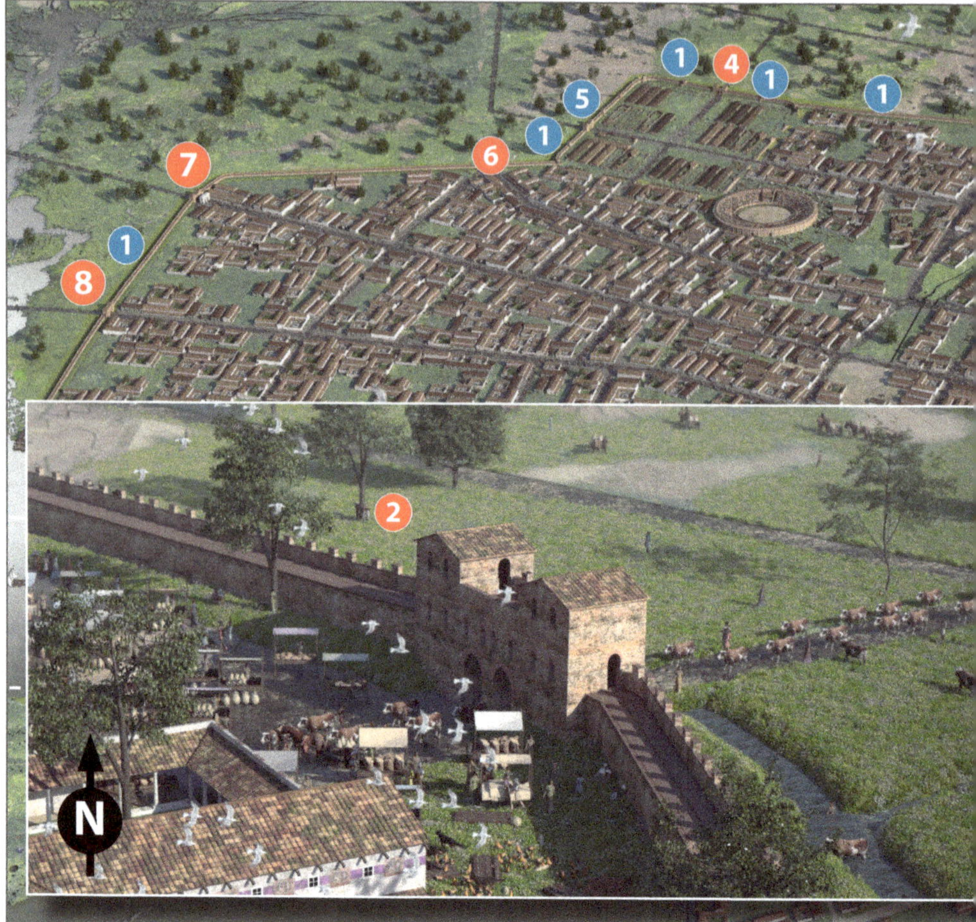

A speculative view of the Roman Town Wall around 245 CE, looking north.

The Roman Town Wall

Around 190-230 CE work was completed on a town wall[1] which encircled Roman London, except the side facing the River Thames. Why it was built is not known, although many Roman towns had extensive defences by this time.

The wall also enclosed the abandoned Roman Fort and had many gatehouses to defend Roman London.

Around 270 CE a defensive wall was added along the side that faced the River Thames, possibly due to increased raids by barbarians. It is thought that an extra gatehouse at Aldersgate was added in the fourth century. In the late 4th century the town wall was upgraded along the east side with around 21 bastions.

1. *See pages 34 to 46 for more details about viewing the Roman Town Wall and gatehouses.*

2. *Bastions were huge stone towers connected to the wall.*

Key

━━ *Roman Town Wall*

▪ ▪ *Roman River Wall 270 CE*

1 *Visible Roman Wall*[1]

2 *Aldgate*

3 *Bishopsgate*

4 *Cripplegate*

5 *Fortress Westgate*

6 *Aldersgate
(4th century)*

7 *Newgate*

8 *Ludgate*

C *The City Wall at
Vine Street Museum*

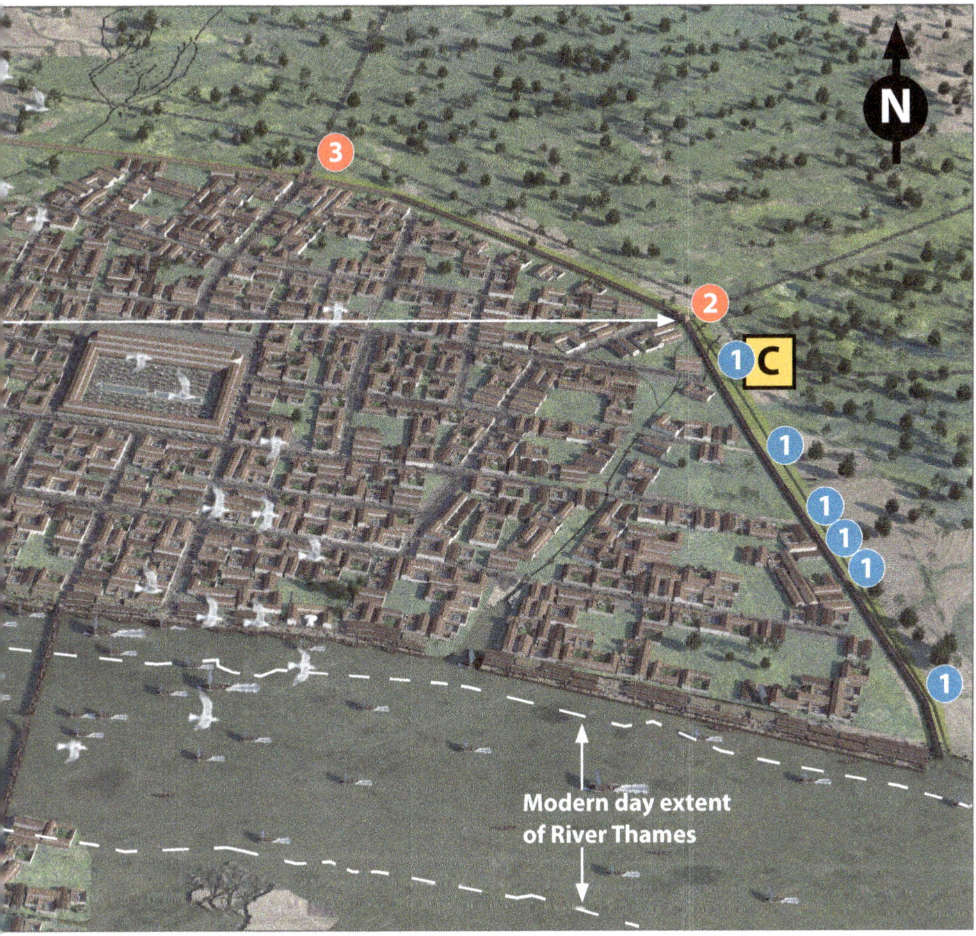

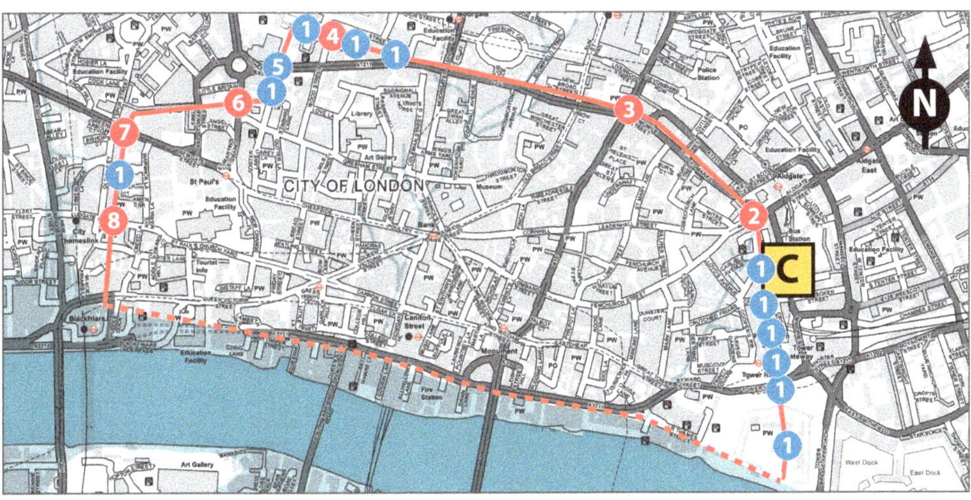

N
3
2
1
C
1
1
1
1
1
Modern day extent
of River Thames

N
1
4
1
1
5
1
6
7
1
8
3
2
1
C
1
1
1
1
1
CITY OF LONDON
St Paul's
Blackfriars
Aldgate
Monument
Cannon Street
Art Gallery
West Dock
East Dock

A speculative view of the Billingsgate Bathhouse around 240 CE, looking north.

The Billingsgate Bathhouse

Most Roman towns had large public bathhouses, where people could bathe and socialise. But for the very wealthy, a private bathhouse was designed to impress. In 1848 a house was found in Billingsgate, which is thought to have been built around 150 CE. A private bathhouse was thought to have been added by the middle of the 3rd century. The bathhouse would have had a furnace to heat a *Caldarium (hot room)*, *Tepidarium (warm room)* and a *Frigidarium (cold room)*. The Romans did not have soap products, so instead used oil and scraped the oil off with a curved implement called a strigil. The bathhouse, located near to the River Thames, may have had many other facilities such as an *Apodyterium (heated changing rooms)*. Firewood for the furnace was probably brought down the River Thames and unloaded next to the bathhouse.

Key

- Roman Wall/Bridge
1. *Private bathhouse*[1]
2. *Caldarium*
3. *Tepidarium*
4. *Frigidarium*
5. *Furnace*
6. *Adjoining house*
7. *Roman quay*
8. *Firewood for furnace*

1. See page 46 for more details about visiting the site.

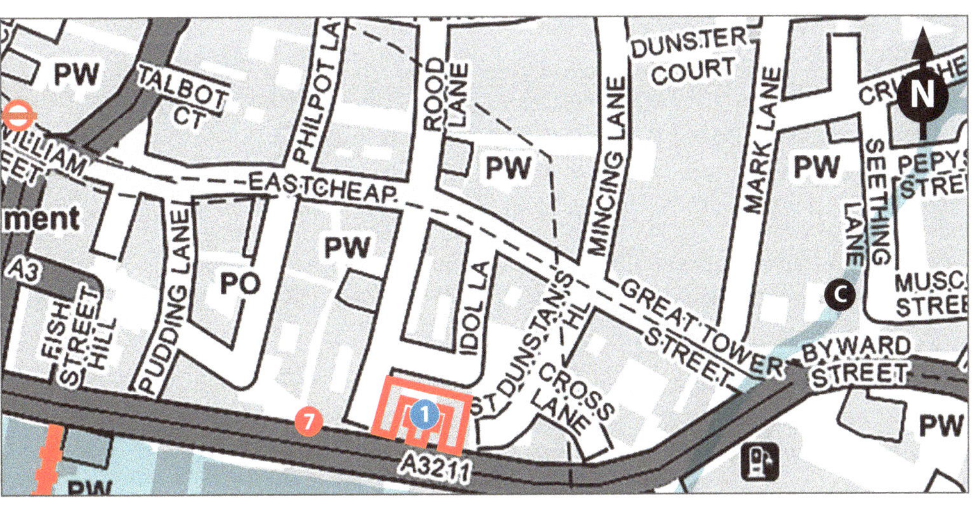

PW
TALBOT CT
PHILPOT LA
ROOD LANE
DUNSTER COURT
MINCING LANE
MARK LANE
CRUTCHE
N
WILLIAM STREET
EASTCHEAP
PW
PW
SEETHING LANE
PEPYS STREE
ment
A3
PO
PUDDING LANE
PW
IDOL LA
ST DUNSTAN'S HL
GREAT TOWER STREET
C
MUSC STREE
FISH STREET HILL
CROSS LANE
BYWARD STREET
PW
7
1
A3211
PW

A speculative view of the Roman Fortress around 130 CE, looking north.

The Roman Fortress

Around 120 CE a large fortress was constructed to the north-west of the Roman town. The fortress was unusual, as usually fortresses were built before a town existed rather than after, as was the case here. This might have meant that London was considered of great importance to Rome. Around 1000 troops may have been based at the fortress, living in purpose built barracks. Most of the layout of the fortress is not known, apart from a few barracks on the south side. The fortress **may** have had similar buildings to those found at Chester, Lincoln and Caerleon. These had granaries, stables, workshops and a *Principia (the administrative hub of a fortress)*. By 200 CE the fortress was no longer in use and had probably fallen into disrepair. The fortress wall was later incorporated into the new town wall *(see page 22)*, although the east and south walls are thought to have been demolished at that time.

Key

- ▬ Roman Fortress Wall
- ▪▪ Future Roman Town Wall
- ① Fortress Wall
- ② Gatehouse
- ③ Gatehouse
- ④ Cripplegate
- ⑤ Barracks
- ⑥ Principia
- ⑦ Granary
- ⑧ Stable block?
- ⑨ Building for officials
- ⑩ Amphitheatre
- Ⓑ Walbrook Stream

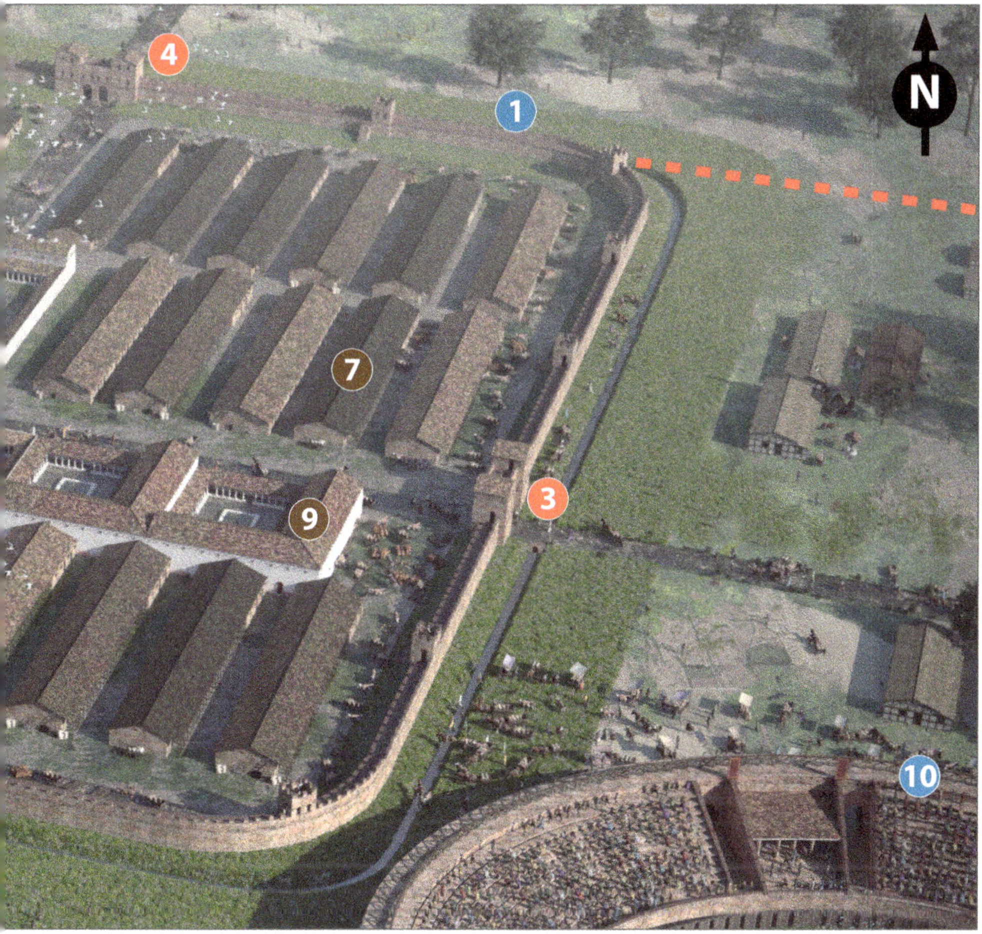

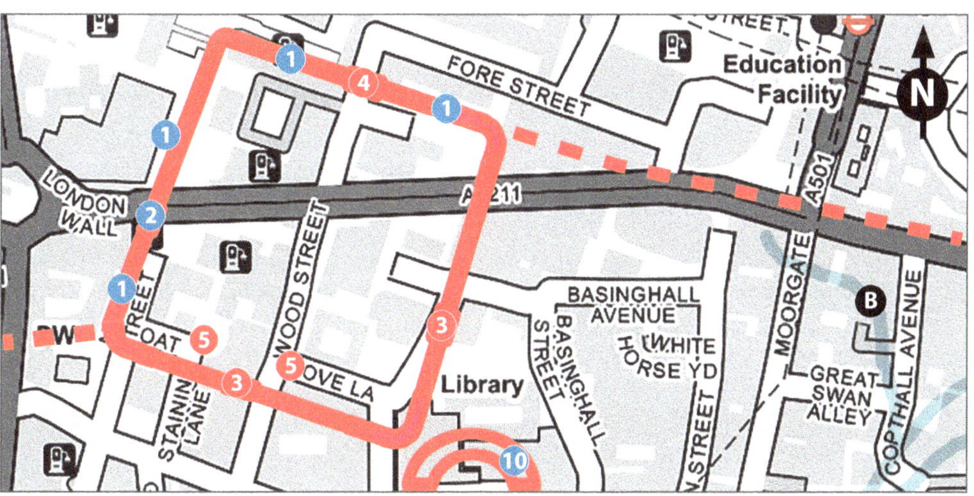

N
4
1
7
3
9
10

FORE STREET
Education Facility
N
4
1
1
1
LONDON WALL
2
STREET
WOOD STREET
A 211
1
MOAT
5
3
5
OVE LA
3
STAINING LANE
Library
BASINGHALL AVENUE
BASINGHALL STREET
WHITE HORSE YD
N. STREET
MOORGATE
A 501
B
GREAT SWAN ALLEY
COPTHALL AVENUE
10

A speculative view of the Roman Port around 230 CE, looking north.

The Roman Port

During Roman times the River Thames was much wider than it is today. After the initial invasion of 43 CE a small port was built to facilitate the supply of military equipment, required by the Roman Legions. Gradually the port was expanded, due to the huge increase in commercial goods. In the decades following the devastating attack by Boudica, the port became a bustling hive of activity, with ships unloading food, wine and much more from all over the Roman Empire. Eventually dedicated quays were built with massive cranes used to unload cargo. This cargo was stored in warehouses which lined the quayside, ready to be sold by wealthy merchants in the vast Basilica/Forum nearby. But the tidal reach of the Thames started to change, making the port less useful, and around 270 CE a large protective wall was built, effectively blocking off the port.

Key

— Roman Town Wall
▬ Line of Roman Bridge
▪ ▪ Line of Roman Quay/
Roman River Wall 270 CE
1 Quay piling[1]
2 Roman Bridge
3 Section of Roman Quay
4 Roman ship
5 Roman warehouse
6 Basilica/Forum

1. Located in front of the Church of Saint Magnus the Martyr (see page 44).

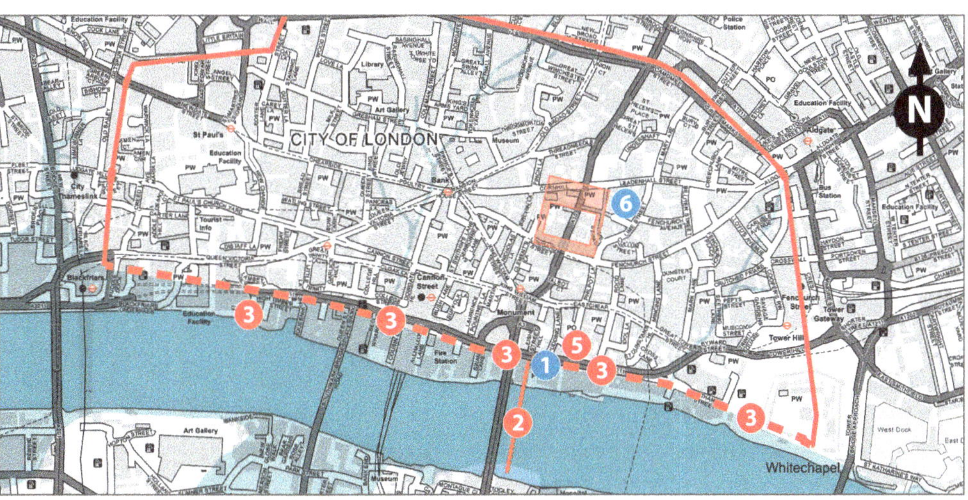

Contains Ordnance Survey data © Crown copyright and database right 2026

A speculative view of the Roman Bridge around 230 CE, looking north.

The Roman Bridge

While the River Thames being so deep and wide had many advantages, trying to cross it was a major technical problem. During the initial invasion of 43 CE the Romans may have used a pontoon bridge[1] to cross the river on their way to Colchester. Then the Romans probably installed a ferry, which was later upgraded into a large wooden bridge. This then helped connect London with other Roman towns connected to the sea, such as Dover. The bridge also connected with a smaller part of Roman London on the south side *(see page 14)*. The bridge possibly had a central drawbridge, to allow seagoing ships to access the western docks. It is thought that the bridge might have been upgraded with a stone version, possibly in the 2nd century.

1. See page 6 for more information.

Key

- Line of wooden Roman Bridge
- **1** Roman Bridge
- Line of Roman Quay
- **2** Section of Roman Quay
- **3** Quay piling[2]
- **4** Roman ship
- **5** Roman warehouse
- **6** Speculated drawbridge

2. A small piece of the Roman Quay is located in front of the Church of Saint Magnus the Martyr (see page 44).

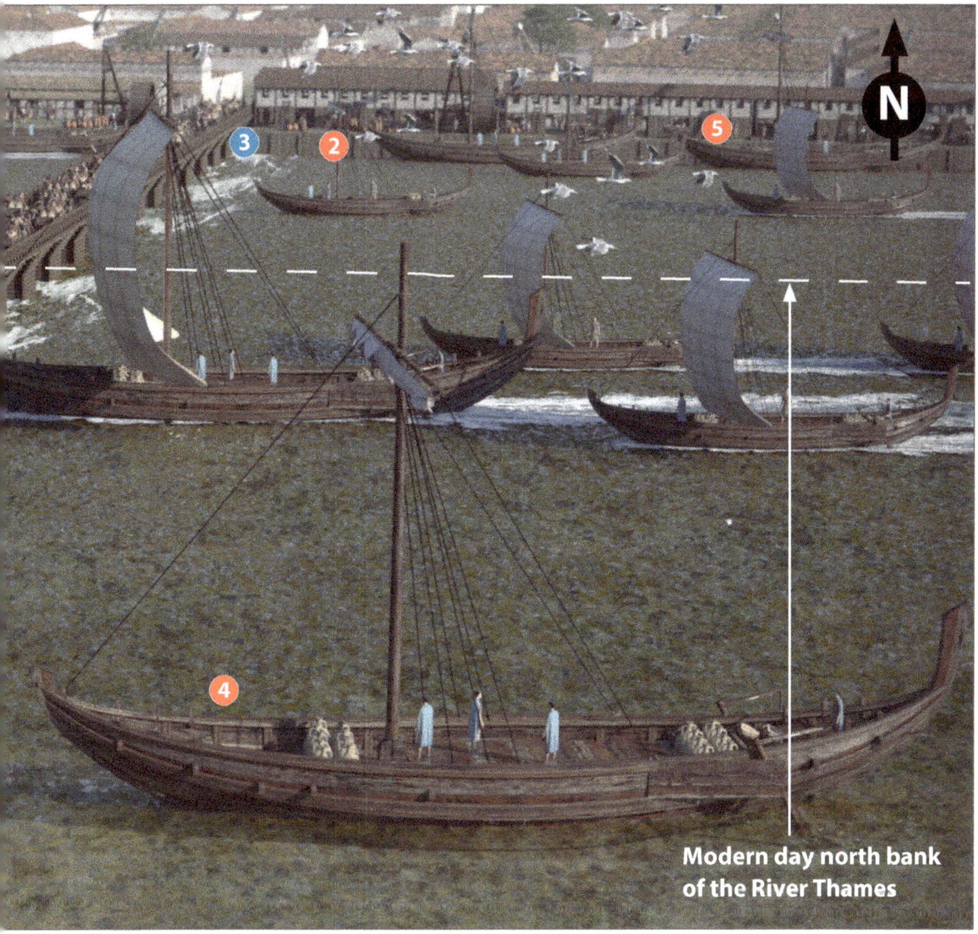

N
Modern day north bank
of the River Thames

BELL WHARF LA
WHARF LA
COUSIN LANE
ALLHALLOWS LANE
Fire
Station
SWAN LANE
LAU
POUN
A3
FISH STREET HILL
PUDDING LA
IDOL LA
PO
PW
PW
ST DUNSTAN'S HILL
CROSS LANE
GREAT T
REE
N
A3211
PW
2
5
3
5
2
1
6

A view showing typical weapons and equipment used by the Second Legion.

The Roman Army

London's history has been interwoven with the Roman Army from the beginning of the Roman invasion in 43 CE. The Thames, at first, proved a barrier for the Roman Army trying to reach Colchester. Once the Thames had been crossed the Romans built a large temporary camp[1], which would have been filled with vast amounts of tents, each housing 8 men. After the initial invasion, equipment for the army was brought in by ships and then sent out across Roman Britain. The Roman Army was almost beaten in 60-61 CE by Boudica and her 120,000 warriors *(see page 10)*, forcing them to abandon London. The image above shows typical equipment used by the *Legio II Augusta (Second Legion 'Augusta')*, one of the four legions deployed during the invasion of 43 CE.

1. See page 6 for more details.

Key

1 *Pilum (Javelin)*
2 *Scutum (Shield)*
3 *Focale (Scarf)*
4 *Gladius (Sword)*
5 *Galea (Helmet)*
6 *Lorica Segmentata (Body Armour)*
7 *Tunica (Tunic)*
8 *Caligae (Sandals)*

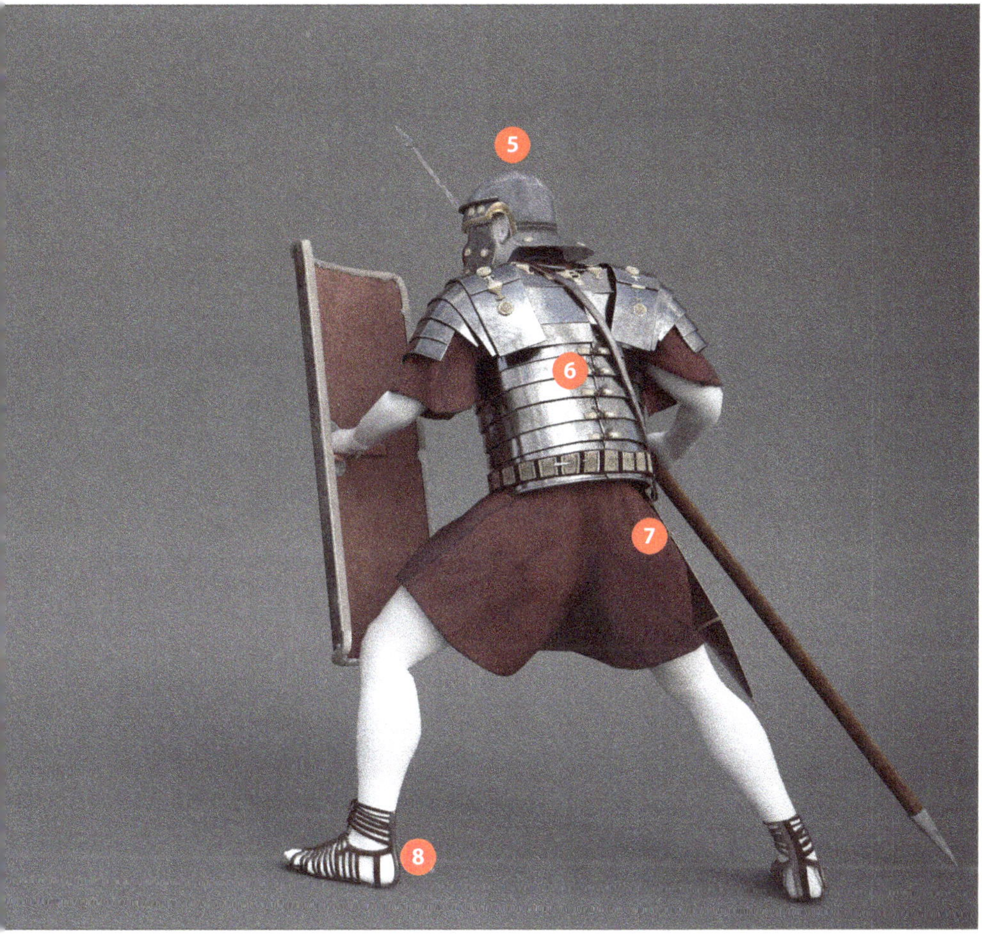

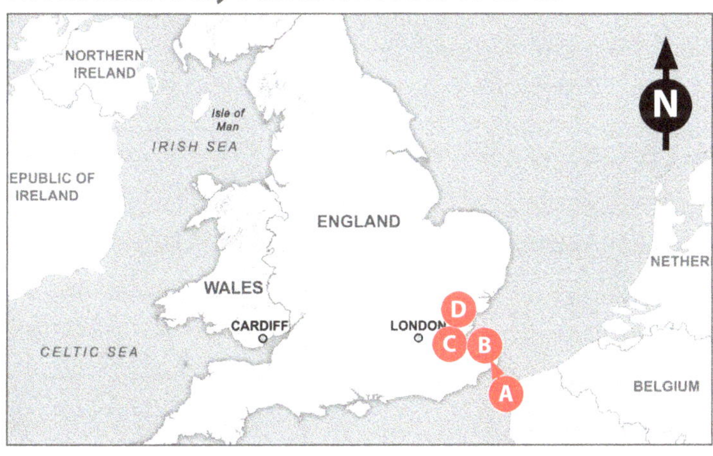

The Roman Army's invasion route of 43 CE

Contains Ordnance Survey data © Crown copyright and database right 2026

- A Boulogne
- B Richborough
- C London area
- D Colchester

The exact point where the Roman Army landed is debated, but it is recorded that the Romans fought local tribes in the London area, before moving towards Colchester.

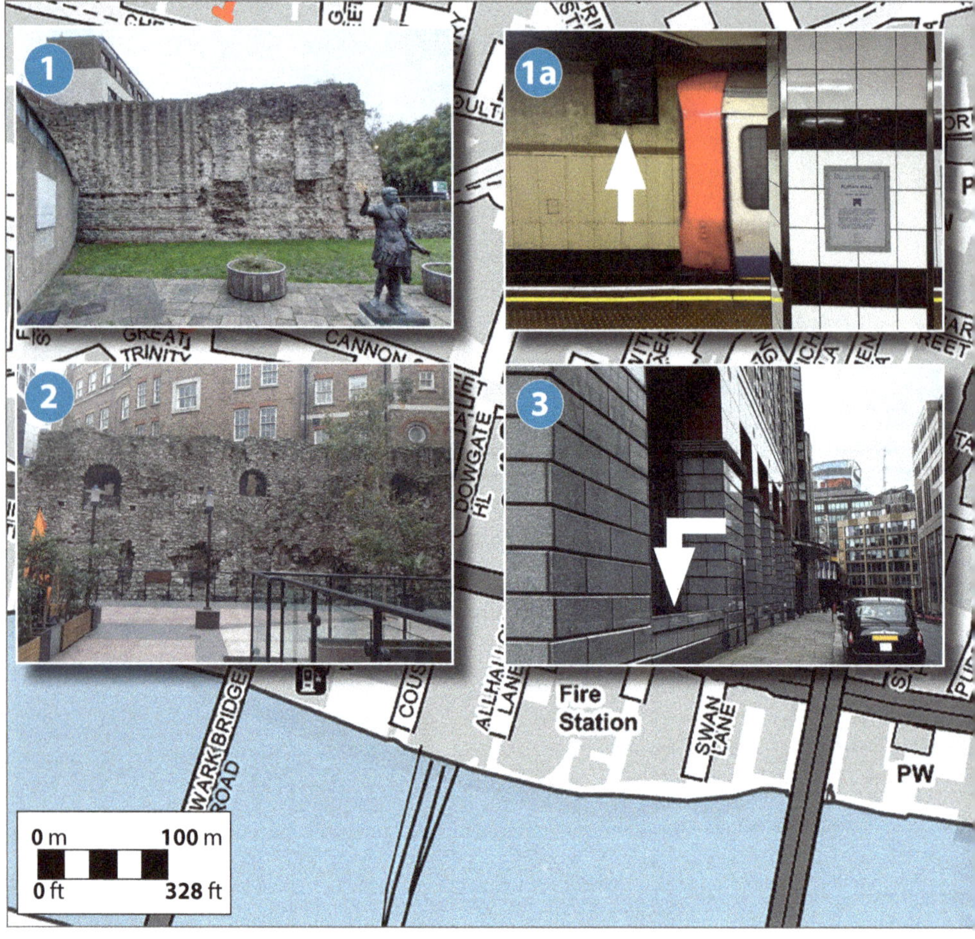

A tour from Tower Hill to Aldgate

Key

— Line of Roman walls
(no visible remains)

🔵 Roman site/wall
(visible remains)

🔴 Roman site/wall
(no visible remains)

C Museum with Roman
artefacts and displays

➤ Route of tour

🔵 **Site of the Roman Town Wall**
(Next to Tower Hill Underground
Station entrance)
• Large section of Roman Town Wall
• Information panels
• Modern sculpture of the Emperor Trajan
• Reconstruction of Roman inscription
found on the site

🔵 **Site of the Roman Town Wall**
(Westbound platform of Tower Hill
Underground Station)
• Very small section of Roman Town Wall
• Information panel

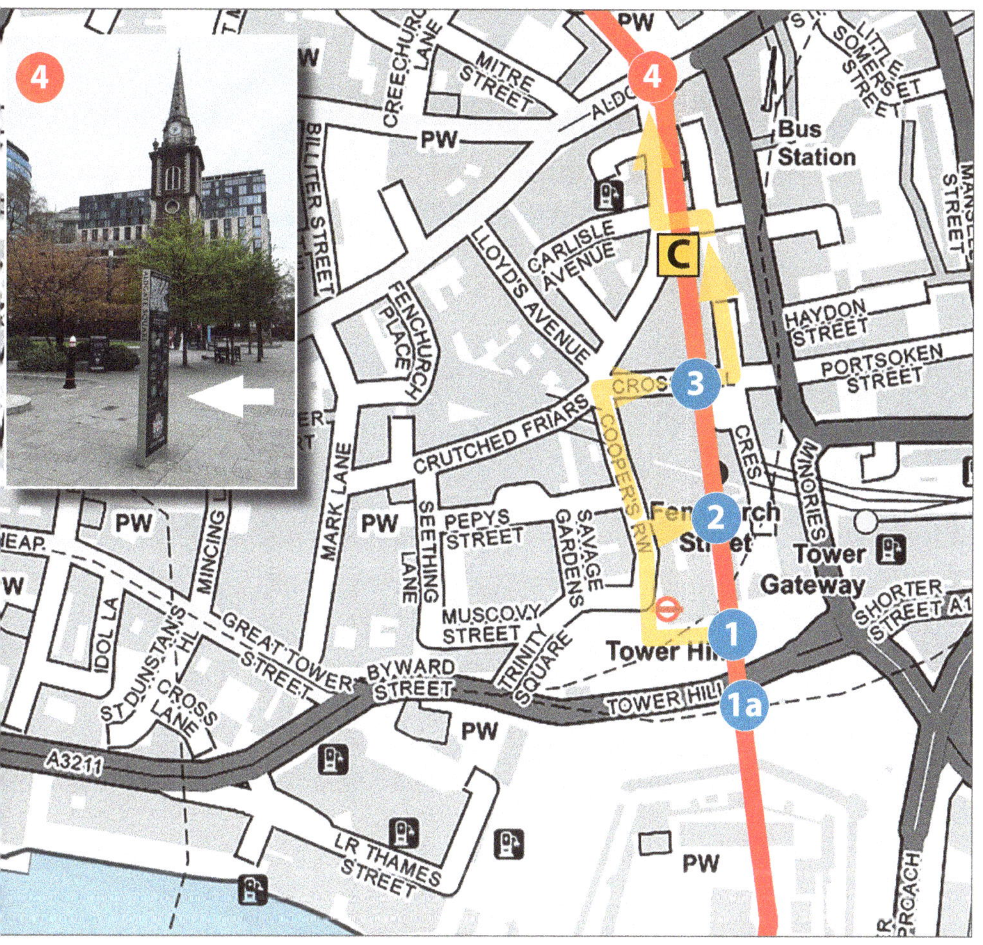

Contains Ordnance Survey data © Crown copyright and database right 2026

2 **Site of the Roman Town Wall**
(In the lobby of the Leonardo Royal Hotel London City, Cooper's Row)
• *Large section of the Roman Town Wall*
• *Information panels*

3 **Site of the Roman Town Wall**
(America One offices, Crosswalk)
Note: Permission is required from security, to view the wall in the lobby. However, it can also be spotted with some difficulty, to the left of the main entrance behind a low grey wall, see white arrow on photograph.
• *Section of Roman Town Wall*

C **Site of the Roman Town Wall**
(City Wall at Vine Street museum)
Free museum *(entrance is on Crouched Friars)*, see online for further details.
• *Large section of the Roman Town Wall*
• *Multiple information panels*
• *Multiple Roman artefacts*

4 **Site of a Roman Gatehouse**
(Aldgate)
(See page 22)
• *Information panel*

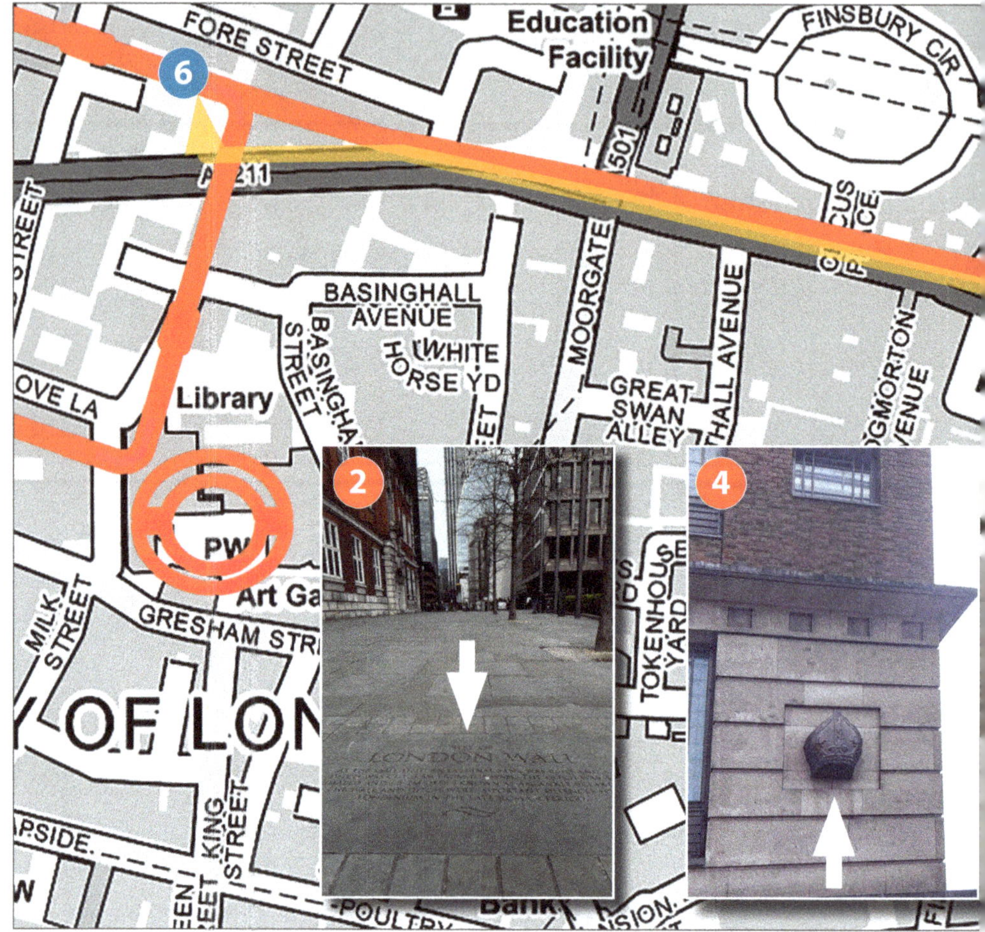

A tour from Aldgate to St Alphage Gardens

Key

— *Line of Roman wall
(no visible remains)*

1 *Roman site/wall
(visible remains)*

1 *Roman site/wall
(no visible remains)*

➤ *Route of tour*

1 **Site of Roman Gatehouse
(Aldgate)**
(See previous page)

2 **Site of the Roman Town Wall
(Aldgate Square, Aldgate)**
• *Information panels inscribed into the
pavement showing the line of the
Roman Town Wall*

3 **Site of the Roman Town Wall
(10-16 Bevis Marks)**
Street following the line of the
Roman Town Wall.
• *Information panel*

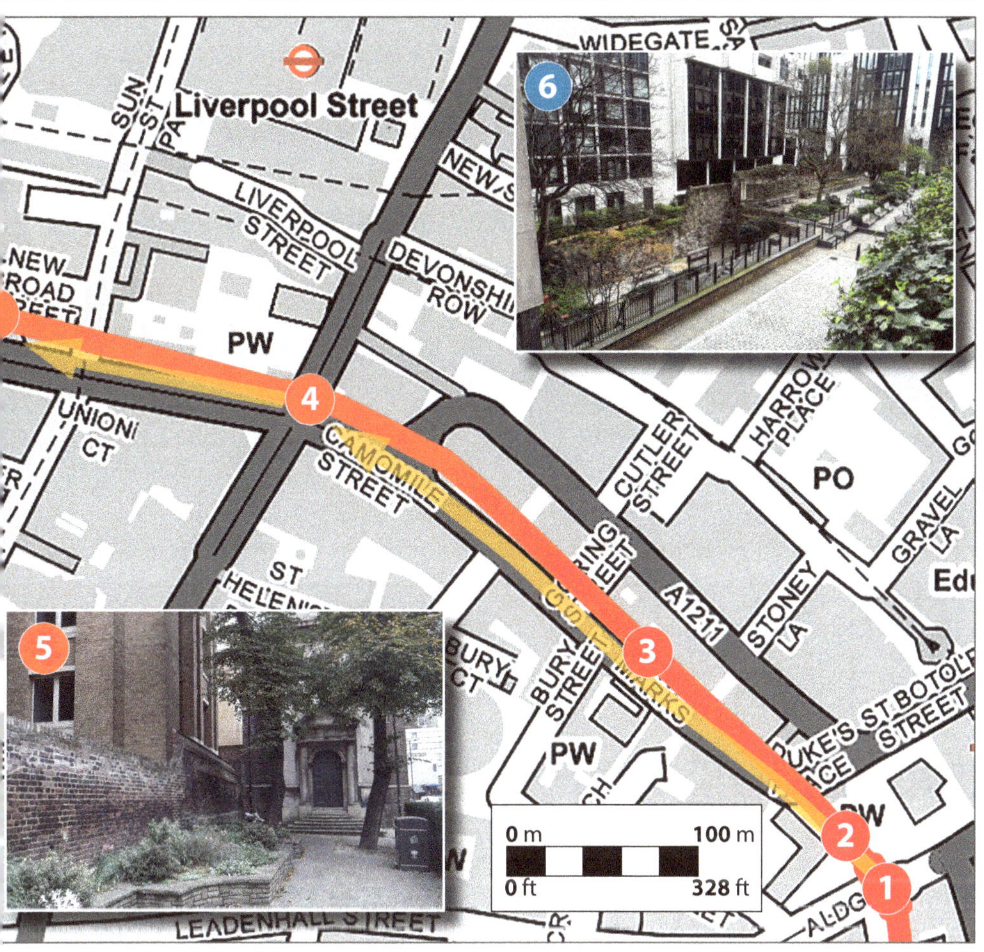

Contains Ordnance Survey data © Crown copyright and database right 2026

4 **Site of Roman Gatehouse**
(Bishopsgate)
A metal bishop's mitre/hat can be seen, marking the position of the gatehouse.

5 **Site of the Roman Town Wall**
(All Hallows-on-the-Wall Church, London Wall)
12th century church built into the Roman Town Wall.
• *No visible remains*

6 **Site of the Roman Fortress Wall**
(St Alphage Gardens, London Wall)
Note the site can be seen at street level and by walking on the Barbican Highwalk. See online for details about how to enter and exit the Barbican Highwalk.
• *Large section of Roman Fortress Wall*
• *Information panels*
• *Gardens, with seating*

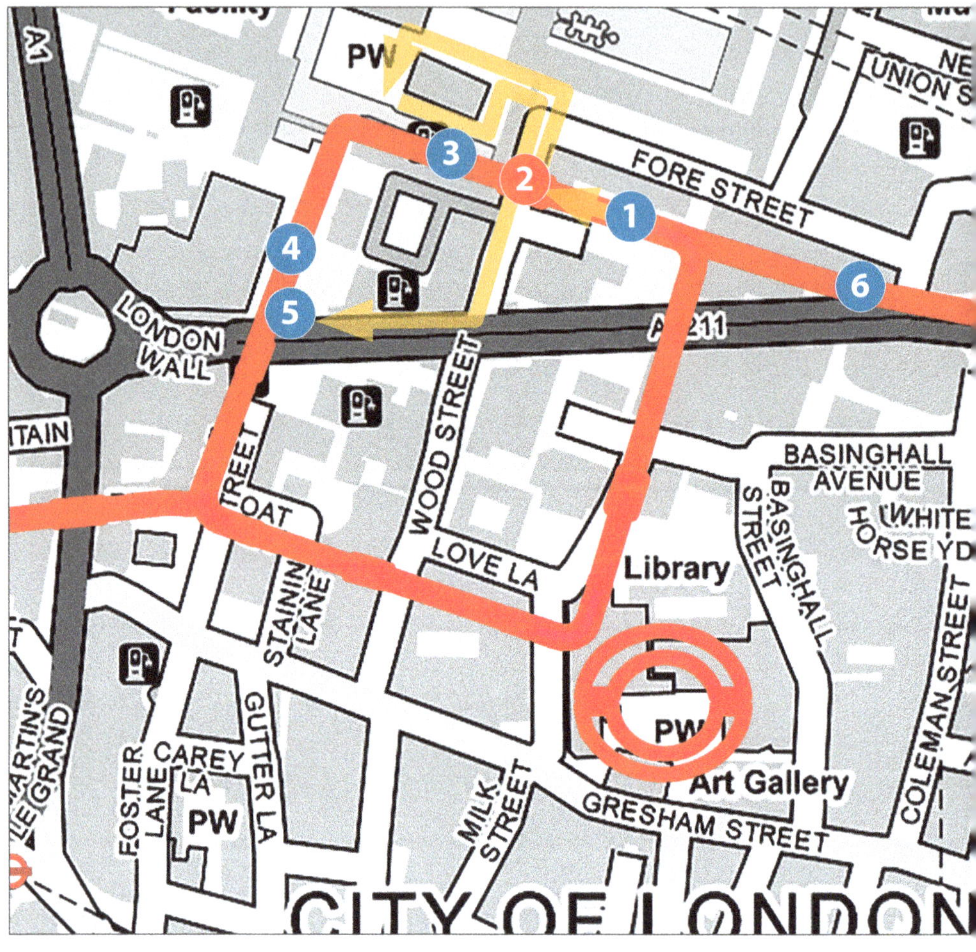

A tour from St Alphage Gdns. to London Wall

Key

— *Line of Roman wall (no visible remains)*

1 *Roman site/wall (visible remains)*

1 *Roman site/wall (no visible remains)*

➤ *Route of tour*

1 **Site of Roman Fortress Wall** ***(St Alphage Gardens, London Wall)*** *(See previous page)*

2 **Site of Roman Fortress Gatehouse** ***(Cripplegate, Wood Street)*** *(See page 26)*
- *Information panel*
- *Blue plaque marking the site*

3 **Site of Roman Fortress Wall** ***(St Giles Cripplegate)*** Note the bastion to the right of the Roman wall is a post-Roman addition.
- *Large section of Roman Fortress Wall*
- *Information panel*

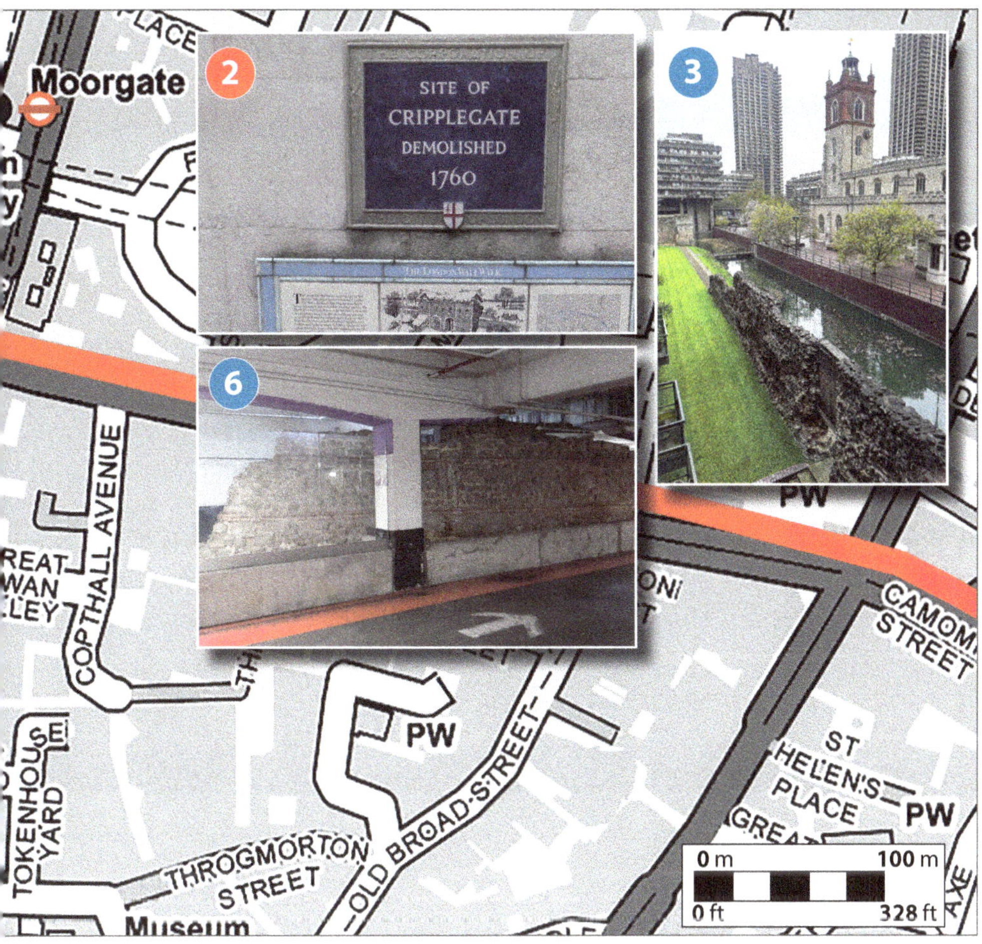

Contains Ordnance Survey data © Crown copyright and database right 2026

4 Section of Roman Fortress Wall (*Barber-Surgeons Gardens*)

Site is difficult to access and obscured by vegetation. Bastions are post-Roman.
- *Section of Roman Fortress Wall*

5 Site of Roman Fortress Gatehouse (*London Wall*)

(See page 26)
- *Section of Roman Fortress Gatehouse*
- *Information panel*
- *Limited tours are offered at certain times of the year by the City of London Corporation, see online for exact details, including where the tour starts from.*

6 Section of Roman Town Wall (*London Wall*)

Visiting this section of the wall involves a ***long*** walk through an underground car park. There are various entrances, some of which can be difficult to find and enter. The entrances to the underground car park are located around 5, see online for exact details.
- *Section of Roman Town Wall*

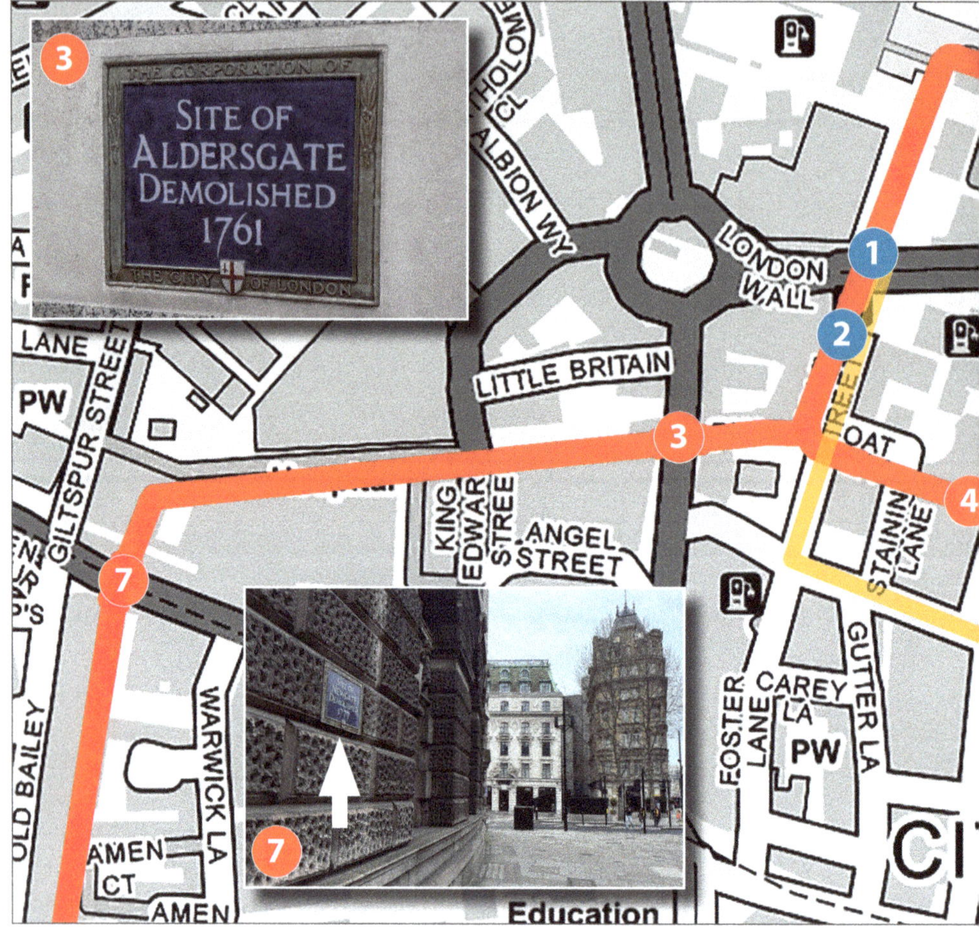

A tour from London Wall to Guildhall Yard

Key

— *Line of Roman wall (no visible remains)*

1 *Roman site/wall (visible remains)*

1 *Roman site/wall (no visible remains)*

A *Museum with Roman artefacts and displays*

➤ *Route of tour*

1 **Site of Roman Fortress Gatehouse**
(*See previous page*)

2 **Section of Roman Fortress Wall (Noble Street)**
Part of the Roman Fortress Wall
• *Large section of the Roman Wall*
• *Information panels*

3 **Site of late Roman Gatehouse (St Martin's Le Grand) Aldersgate**
(*See page 22*)
• *Blue plaque marking the site*

4 **Site of Roman Fortress Gatehouse (Wood Street)**
(*See page 26*)
• *No visible remains*

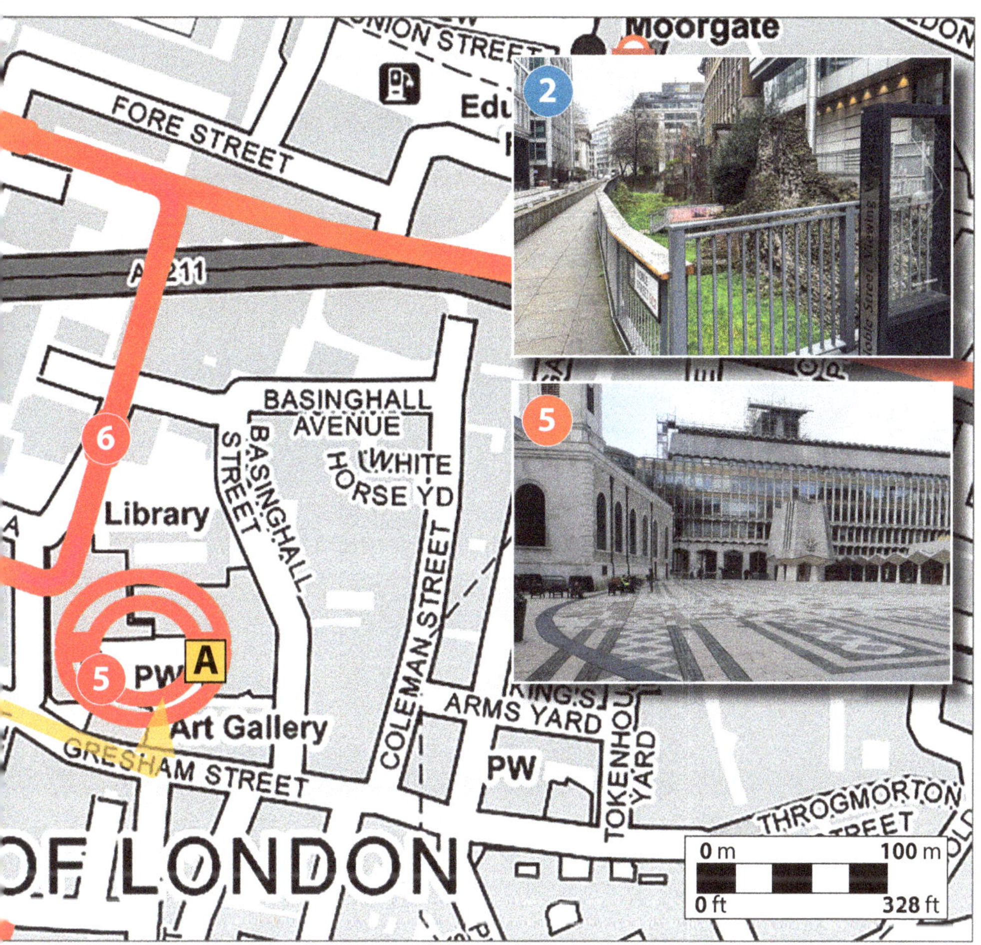

Contains Ordnance Survey data © Crown copyright and database right 2026

5 **Site of the Roman Amphitheatre**
(Guildhall Yard)
- *The outline of the amphitheatre is*
  marked in the courtyard, with black tiles

A **Guildhall Art Gallery and**
Roman Amphitheatre (Guildhall Yard)
Large free museum, see online for
further details. *(See page 16 for more*
about the amphitheatre.)
- *Extensive sections of the*
  Roman Amphitheatre
- *Extensive information panels*
- *Multiple Roman artefacts*
- *Gift shop*

6 **Site of Roman Fortress Gatehouse**
(Aldermanbury)
(See page 26)
- *No visible remains*

7 **Site of Roman Gatehouse**
(Newgate)
(See page 22)
- *Blue plaque marking the site*

A tour from Guildhall Yard to Walbrook

Key

— *Line of Roman wall (no visible remains)*

1 *Roman site/wall (visible remains)*

1 *Roman site/wall (no visible remains)*

A *Museum with Roman artefacts and displays*

➤ *Route of tour*

A Site of the Roman Amphitheatre *(Guildhall Art Gallery and Roman Amphitheatre, Guildhall Yard)* (See previous page)

E Bank of England Museum *(Bartholomew Lane)* Free museum, see online for further details.

• *Roman artefacts*

• *Gift shop*

1 The Bucklersbury Pavement *(Queen Victoria Street)* A Roman mosaic was discovered here in 1869, see online for further details.

• *No visible remains.*

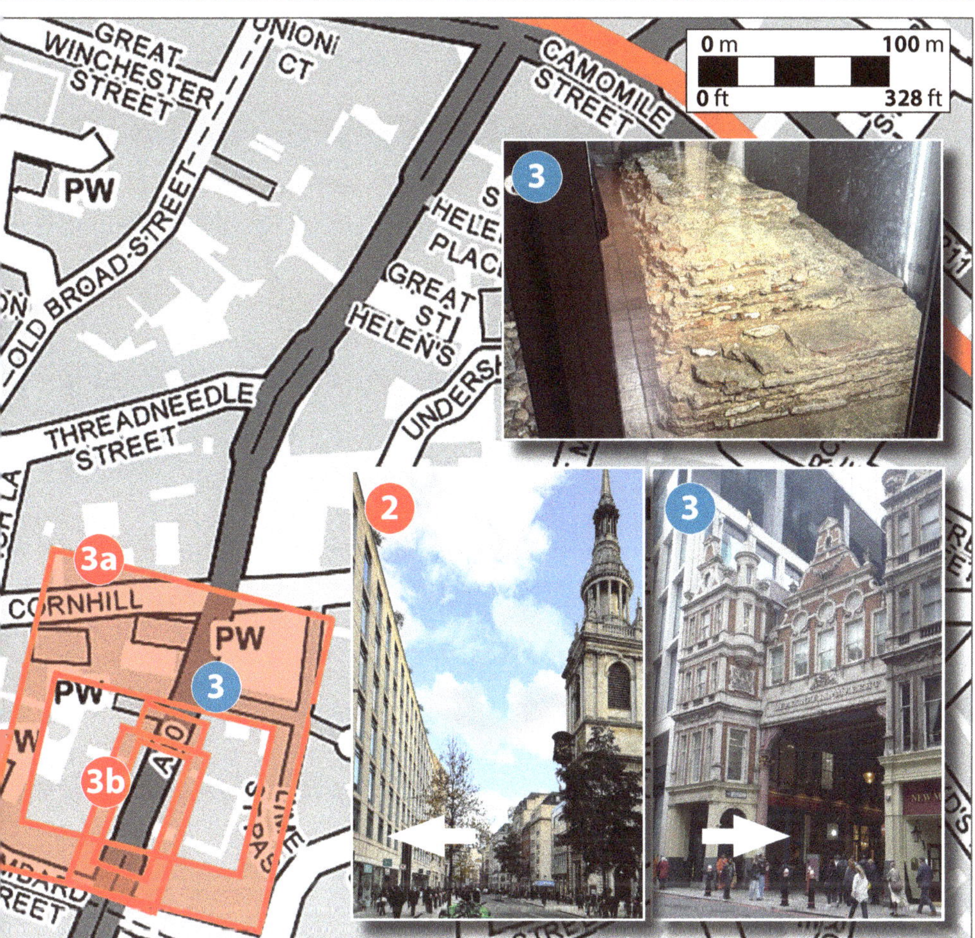

Contains Ordnance Survey data © Crown copyright and database right 2026

2 Roman Public Bathhouse *(Cheapside)*
Site of a Roman Public Roman
Bathhouse, discovered in 1955.
• *No visible remains*

B Site of Roman Mithraeum
**(*London Mithraeum|Bloomberg SPACE,*
Walbrook)**
Free museum displaying a Mithraeum,
see online for further details.
(See page 18 for more about the site.)
• *Extensive section of Mithraeum (temple)*
• *Light show*
• *Roman artefacts*
• *Information panels*

3 Site of the later Basilica/Forum
**(*Leadenhall Market,*
Gracechurch Street)**
(See page 20 for more about the site.)
• *A section of the later Basilica can be
viewed in the basement of Chango
Empanadas, inside Leadenhall Market
(see white arrow on photograph).*
*Note: Special permission is required from
the owners to access the basement.*
3a *Outline of later Basilica/Forum*
3b *Outline of first Basilica/Forum*

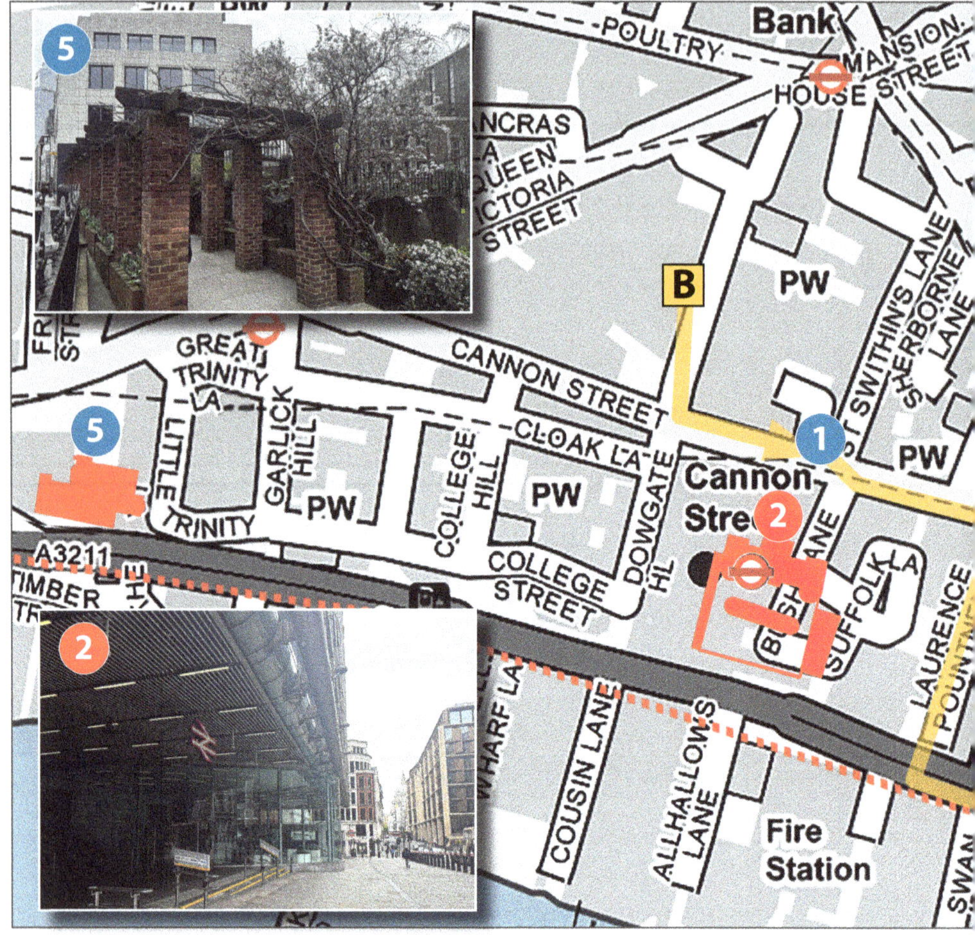

A tour from Walbrook to Lower Thames St.

Key

- ▬ *Line of Roman wall (no visible remains)*
- ▪▪ *Roman quay/wall (no visible remains)*
- ⬌ *Line of Roman bridge (no visible remains)*
- ① *Roman site/wall (visible remains)*
- ① *Roman site/wall (no visible remains)*
- **B** *Museum with Roman artefacts and displays*
- ➤ *Route of tour*

B **Site of Roman Mithraeum**
(London Mithraeum|Bloomberg SPACE, Walbrook)
(*See previous page*)

① **Site of the 'London Stone'**
(Cannon Street/Salter Hall Court)
A small section of stone masonry, thought to be Roman, but now known as the London Stone. Its fate is said to be linked with London's.
• *Possible Roman artefact*
• *Information panel*

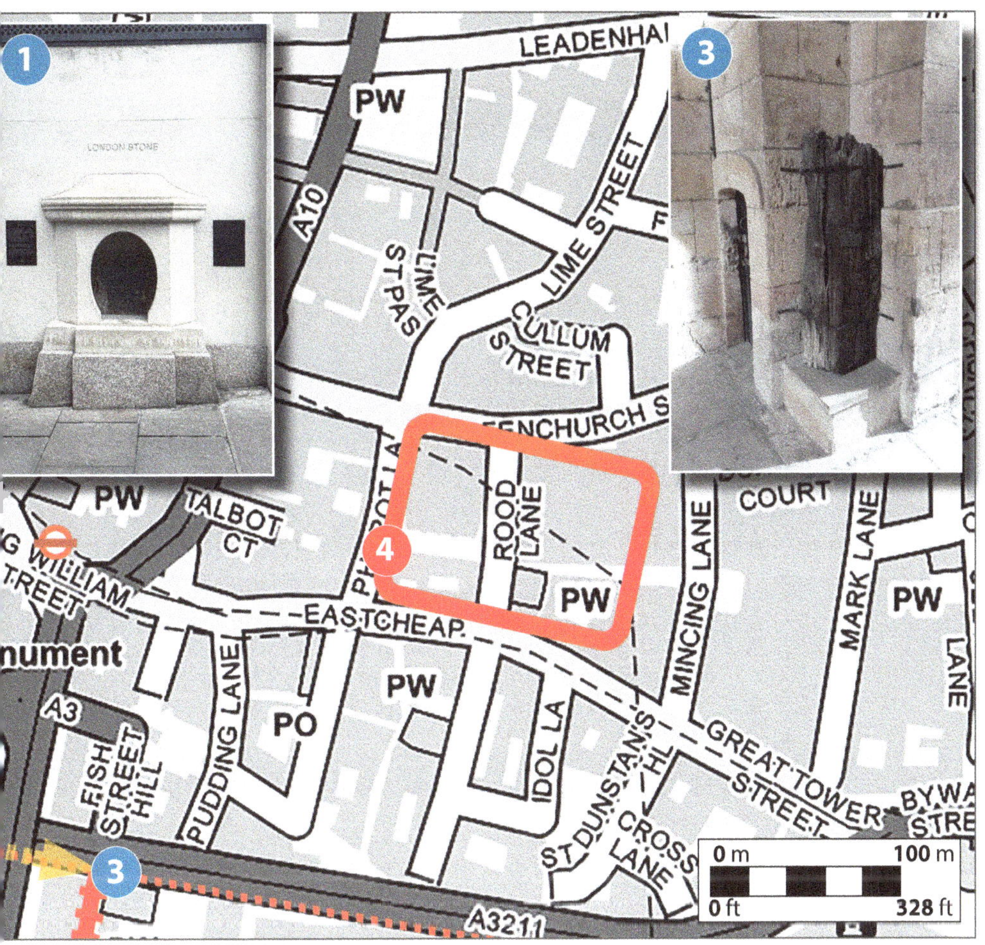

Contains Ordnance Survey data © Crown copyright and database right 2026

2 **Site of the Roman *'Governor's Palace'* (*Cannon Street*)**

Originally thought to be a palace for the Governor of Roman Britain, now thought to have been a large public bathhouse. *(See page 14)*

• *No visible remains*

3 **Section of the Roman Quay (*North side of the Church of Saint Magnus-the-Martyr, Lower Thames Street, Fish Street Hill*)**

(See page 28 for more details about the site).

• *Small section of the Roman Quay (wood)*
• *Small information panel*

4 **Site of a Post-Boudica Fortress (*Rood Lane*)**

A small temporary fortress was built here after the devastating attack by Boudica *(see page 10)*.

• *No visible remains*

5 **Site of Roman Public Bathhouse (*Cleary Garden, Huggin Hill*)**

Site of a public Roman Bathhouse, discovered in 1964. *(See page 14)*

• *Online sources show visible remains, but they now seem to be obscured with vegetation.*

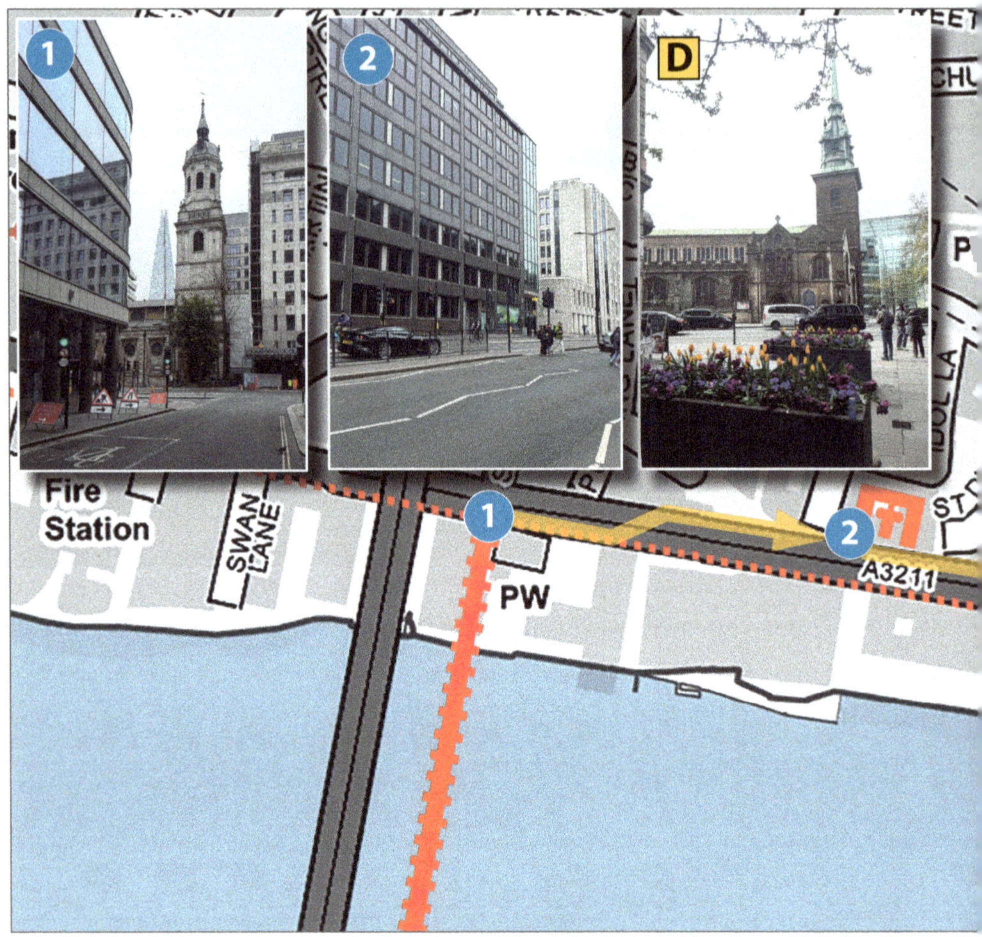

A tour from Lower Thames St. to Tower Hill

Key

- ▬ *Line of Roman wall (no visible remains)*
- ▬ ▬ *Line of Roman quay and later Riverside wall (no visible remains)*
- ▬ *Line of Roman bridge (no visible remains)*
- ① *Roman site/wall (visible remains)*
- ① *Roman site/wall (no visible remains)*
- D *Museum with Roman artefacts and displays*
- ➤ *Route of tour*

① **Section of the Roman Quay (North side of the Church of Saint Magnus-the-Martyr, Lower Thames Street, Fish Street Hill)**
(See previous page)

② **Site of Roman Public Bathhouse (Billingsgate Roman House & Baths, Lower Thames Street/Old Billingsgate Walk)**
(See page 24 for more about the site)
- *Tours available at certain times of the year, check online for details*
- *Extensive section of Roman Bathhouse*
- *Information panels*

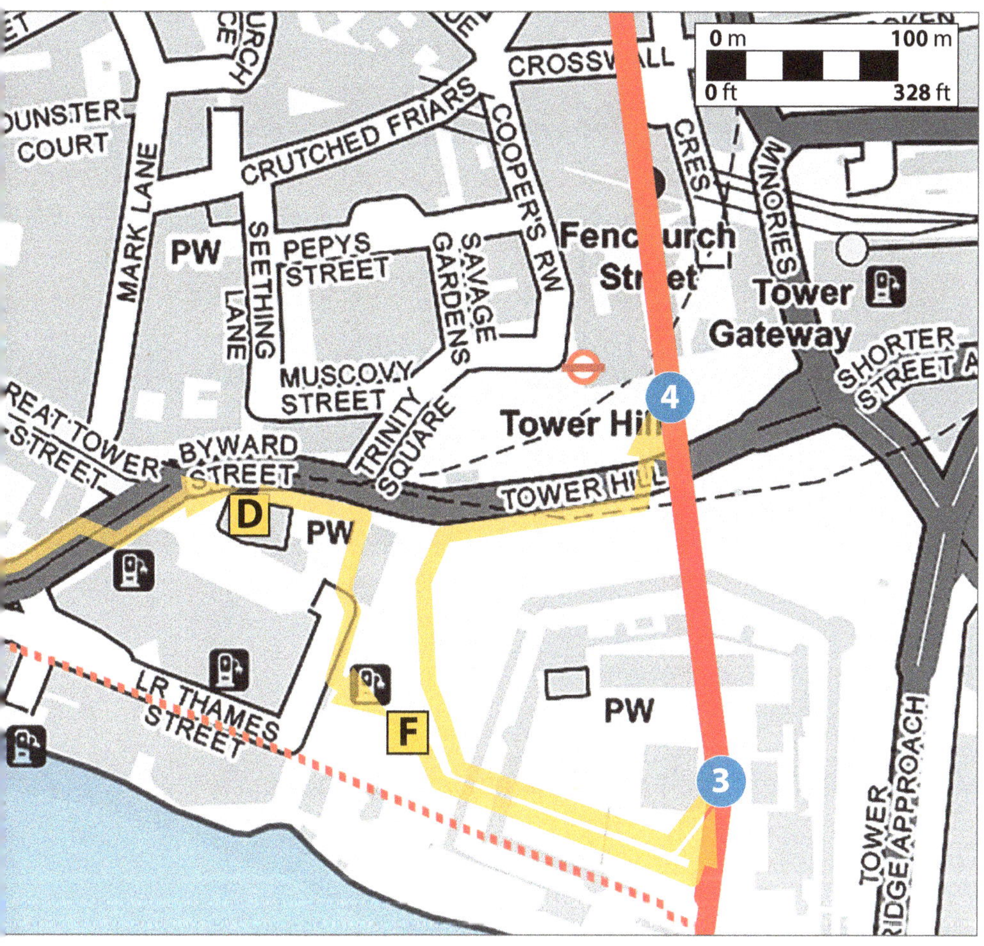

Contains Ordnance Survey data © Crown copyright and database right 2026

D The Crypt Museum & Undercroft, All Hallows by the Tower
(Byward Street/Seething Lane)

Free museum in the basement of a church.

- *Roman artefacts*
- *Information panels*
- *Model of Roman London*

F The Tower of London
(West Entrance on Petty Wales)

A section of the Roman Town Wall can be seen in the Tower of London Grounds, but an entrance fee is required to gain access.

3 Roman Town Wall and Bastion
(The Tower of London)

- *Roman Town Wall and Roman Bastion*
- *Information panels*
- *Outline of the Roman Town Wall*

4 Site of the Roman Town Wall
(Next to Tower Hill Underground Station entrance)

- *Large section of Roman Town Wall*
- *Information panels*
- *Modern sculpture of the Emperor Trajan*
- *Reconstruction of Roman inscription found on the site*

The legacy of the Romans in London

Key

— *Area covered in the preceding sections of this guide*

G *Museum with Roman artefacts and displays*

1 *Roman site (visible remains)*

1 *Modern artefact inspired by the Romans*

The Roman influence

Present day London has many buildings and statues that are clearly influenced by its Roman past. A small selection are shown here that can be seen while walking around London.

In addition, London has many fine museums that feature Roman artefacts, outside the City of London. These museums are shown on this map, please see online for specific locations and opening times.

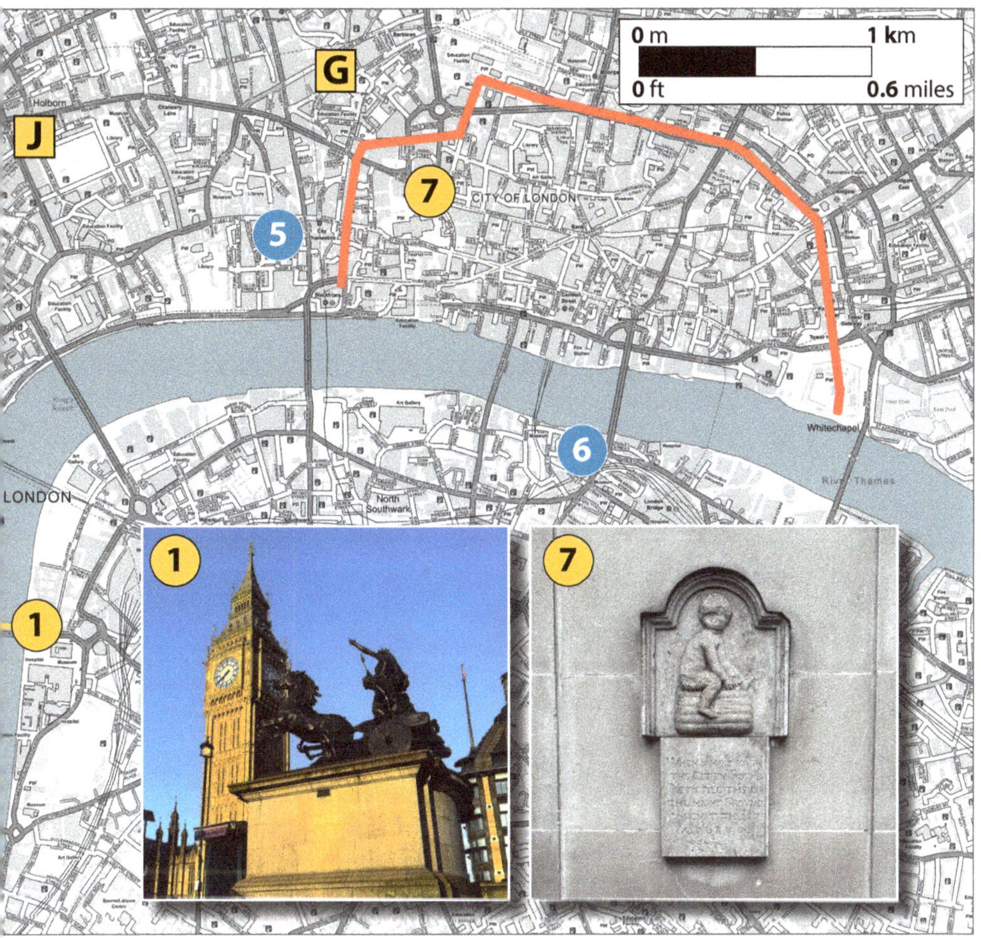

Contains Ordnance Survey data © Crown copyright and database right 2026

G **The British Museum**
Internationally renowned museum with an extensive collection of Roman artefacts.

H **London Museum**
Due to open late 2026, the museum will have many artefacts from Roman London.

I **The Victoria and Albert Museum**
A selection of Roman artefacts from the Roman world.

J **Sir John Soane's Museum**
A selection of Roman artefacts.

1 **Boadicea (Boudica) and Her Daughters**
1902 statue, next to Westminster Bridge.

2 **The Huntress Fountain (Hyde Park)**
1906 statue, of the Roman goddess: Diana.

3 **King James II (Trafalgar Square)**
1686 statue, of the king in Roman clothing.

4 **Wellington Arch (Hyde Park Corner)**
Completed in 1913, it has many Roman and classical influences, including a quadriga (a chariot pulled by four horses).

5 **St. Bride's Church, Fleet Street**
A small selection of Roman artefacts.

6 **Southwark Cathedral**
A small selection of Roman artefacts.

7 **Panyer Boy (Panyer Alley)**
This 1688 bas-relief mentions that the local area is the highest point in the City of London, suggesting that is why the Romans built Londinium here.

Gigantic computer models were used to produce the illustrations in this book.

Behind the scenes

Bringing Roman London to life was a massive project. The first stage involved a significant amount of research, studying maps, books, contacting experts, site visits and much more.

All of this preparation was required to build a gigantic computer model of London in Roman times. This model involved modelling *(or purchasing computer models)* of hundreds of different objects including: *Public buildings, houses, ships, roads, people, animals, buckets, and grass.*

All of these models had to have textures *(such as wood or stone)* added, before being rendered in vast scenes, like the one above.

Then special effects such as water, fire and dust were all added, to bring the past to life. Once the images were produced they were arranged in the book alongside simple annotations and maps, to allow the reader to easily compare the past with the present. Although the maps look simple, a large amount of experimentation was undertaken to effectively convey complex archaeological data overlayed on modern maps. All of these elements were combined into this book, designed to be small enough to use as a pocket guide while visiting London and also provide a souvenir afterwards.

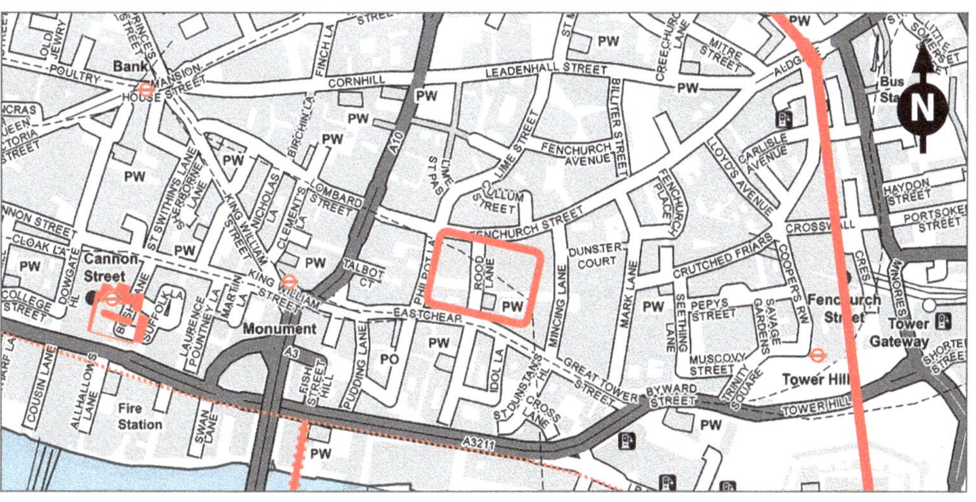
OLD JEWRY
PRINCES STREET
POULTRY
Bank
MANSION HOUSE STREET
CORNHILL
FINCH LA
STREET
LEADENHALL STREET
ST M
PW
CREECHURCH LANE
MITRE STREET
PW
ALDG
PW
LITTLE SOMERSET
Bus Sta
N
PCRAS
QUEEN VICTORIA STREET
BIRCHIN LA
PW
PW
A10
LIME ST PAS
LIME STREET
FENCHURCH AVENUE
BILLITER STREET
PW
LLOYD'S AVENUE
CARLISLE AVENUE
HAYDON STREET
CANNON STREET
CLOAK LA
PW
ST SWITHIN'S LANE
SHERBORNE LANE
KING NICHOLAS LA
LOMBARD STREET
CLEMENT'S LANE
PULLUM STREET
FENCHURCH STREET
FENCHURCH PLACE
CROSSWALL
PORTSOKEN STREET
PW
Cannon Street
DOWGATE HILL
KING WILLIAM STREET
MARTIN LA
TALBOT CT
PHILPOT LA
ROOD LANE
DUNSTER COURT
MARK LANE
CRUTCHED FRIARS
COOPER'S RW
MINORIES CRES
Fenchurch Street
COLLEGE STREET
LAURENCE POUNTNEY LA
KING WILLIAM STREET
EASTCHEAP
PW
MINCING LANE
PW
SEETHING LANE
PEPYS STREET
SAVAGE GARDENS
Tower Gateway
Monument
A3
FISH STREET HILL
PUDDING LANE
IDOL LA
ST DUNSTAN'S HL
GREAT TOWER STREET
MUSCOVY STREET
TRINITY SQUARE
SHORTER
PO
Tower Hill
WHARF LANE
COUSIN LANE
ALLHALLOWS LANE
SWAN LANE
Fire Station
ST DUNSTAN'S CROSS LANE
BYWARD STREET
TOWER HILL
PW
A3211
PW

JC3DVIS
PUBLISHING

First published July 2024. ISBN 978-1-7391254-9-3 *(Paperback)*
Second Edition. Designed and published by JC3DVIS. www.jc3dvis.co.uk
Book design and illustrations © 2026 Joseph Chittenden/JC3DVIS

With special thanks to:
Chiz Harwood: *Senior Archaeologist and Project Officer at the Museum of London*
Archaeology Service from 1998-2008

Dr Dominic Perring: *Director, Centre for Applied Archaeology at University College*
London, Author of Roman London, Oxford University Press
Check out Historic VR 'Londinium AD 215 on Steam

Jane Chittenden: *Proofreading, research, publishing consultancy*

Chango Empanadas, Leadenhall Market, for allowing the author to view the ruins of
the Roman Basilica

Legal disclaimer

Bibliography and sources *(partial list)*
• All Hallows by the Tower museum *(Museum visit)*
• Connolly. P: *The Ancient City*
• Goldsworthy. A: *The Complete Roman Army*
• Hall. J and Merrifield. R: *Roman London*
• https://www.heritagegateway.org.uk/Gateway/Results_Single.aspx?uid=cef95e6c-
  7cb9-4c06-a345-8e67fa3ae5d0&resourceID=19191 *(London Governor's Palace)*
• London Mithraeum, Bloomberg SPACE *(Museum visit)*
• Marsden. P: *Reconstructing the forum and basilica of Roman London (accessed online)*
• Milne. G: *The Port of London*
• Milne. G: *Roman London*
• Ordnance Survey: *Londinium*
• Roman Amphitheatre, Guildhall Art Gallery *(Museum visit)*
• Roman Wall information panels *(accessed online)*
• The City Wall at Vine Street *(Museum visit)*
• Various: *Archaeology at Bloomberg (accessed online)*